Psychology Express

Research Methods
in Psychology

The PsychologyExpress series

→ **UNDERSTAND QUICKLY**
→ **REVISE EFFECTIVELY**
→ **TAKE EXAMS WITH CONFIDENCE**

'All of the revision material I need in one place – a must for psychology undergrads.'
Andrea Franklin, Psychology student at Anglia Ruskin University

'Very useful, straight to the point and provides guidance to the student, while helping them to develop independent learning.'
Lindsay Pitcher, Psychology student at Anglia Ruskin University

'Engaging, interesting, comprehensive . . . it helps to guide understanding and boosts confidence.'
Megan Munro, Forensic Psychology student at Leeds Trinity University College

'Very useful . . . bridges the gap between Statistics textbooks and Statistics workbooks.'
Chris Lynch, Psychology student at the University of Chester

'The answer guidelines are brilliant, I wish I had had it last year.'
Tony Whalley, Psychology student at the University of Chester

'I definitely would (buy a revision guide) as I like the structure, the assessment advice and practice questions and would feel more confident knowing exactly what to revise and having something to refer to.'
Steff Copestake, Psychology student at the University of Chester

'The clarity is absolutely first rate . . . These chapters will be an excellent revision guide for students as well as providing a good opportunity for novel forms of assessment in and out of class.'
Dr Deaglan Page, Queen's University, Belfast

'Do you think they will help students when revising/working towards assessment? Unreservedly, yes.'
Dr Mike Cox, Newcastle University

'The revision guide should be very helpful to students preparing for their exams.'
Dr Kun Guo, University of Lincoln

'A brilliant revision guide, very helpful for students of all levels.'
Svetoslav Georgiev, Psychology student at Anglia Ruskin University

Research Methods in Psychology

Steve Jones
Leeds Trinity University College

Mark Forshaw
Staffordshire University

Series editor:
Dominic Upton
University of Worcester

Psychology Express

Prentice Hall
is an imprint of

Harlow, England • London • New York • Boston • San Francisco • Toronto
Sydney • Tokyo • Singapore • Hong Kong • Seoul • Taipei • New Delhi
Cape Town • Madrid • Mexico City • Amsterdam • Munich • Paris • Milan

Pearson Education Limited
Edinburgh Gate
Harlow
Essex CM20 2JE
England

and Associated Companies throughout the world

Visit us on the World Wide Web at:
www.pearson.com/uk

First published 2012

ISBN 978-0-273-73725-4

British Library Cataloguing-in-Publication Data
A catalogue record for this book is available from the British Library

Library of Congress Cataloging-in-Publication Data
A catalog record for this book is available from the Library of Congress

10 9 8 7 6 5 4 3 2 1
15 14 13 12 11

Typeset in 9.5/12.5pt Avenir Book by 30
Printed in Great Britain by Henry Ling Ltd, at the Dorset Press, Dorchester, Dorset

Contents

Supporting resources

Visit www.pearsoned.co.uk/psychologyexpress to find valuable online resources.

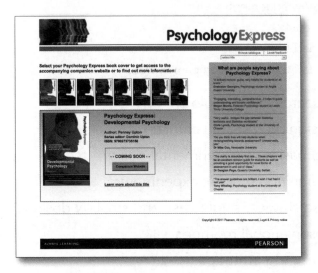

Companion website for students

→ **Get help in organising your revision**: download and print topic maps and revision checklists for each area.

→ **Ensure you know the key concepts in each area**: test yourself with flashcards. You can use them online, print them out or download to an iPod.

→ **Improve the quality of your essays in assignments and exams**: use the sample exam questions, referring to the answer guidelines for extra help.

→ **Practise for exams**: check the answers to the Test your knowledge sections in this book and take additional tests for each chapter.

→ **Go into exams with confidence**: use the You be the marker exercises to consider sample answers through the eyes of the examiner.

Also: The companion website provides the following features:

● Search tool to help locate specific items of content.

● E-mail results and profile tools to send results of quizzes to instructors.

● Online help and support to assist with website usage and troubleshooting.

For more information please contact your local Pearson Education sales representative or visit **www.pearsoned.co.uk/psychologyexpress**.

Acknowledgements

Authors' acknowledgements

Steve Jones: Thanks to Alison, Laura and Philip for being there and for not asking too many difficult questions about what I was doing.

Mark Forshaw: Thanks to Steve Jones, for his patient responses every time I forgot what I was doing. Thanks to Amanda Crowfoot, just because.

Both: Thanks to Dominic Upton for inviting us to engage with this series of books.

Series editor's acknowledgments

I am grateful to Janey Webb and Jane Lawes at Pearson Education for their assistance with this series. I would also like to thank Penney, Francesca, Rosie and Gabriel for their dedication to psychology.

Dominic Upton

Publisher's acknowledgements

Our thanks go to all the reviewers who contributed to the development of this text, including students who participated in research and focus groups, which helped to shape the series format:

Dr Johan Braeken, Tilburg University, the Netherlands
Dr Mike Cox, Newcastle University
Professor Simona Gaarthuis, Hogeschool van Amsterdam, the Netherlands
Professor Marion Kloep, University of Glamorgan
Dr Angela Nananidou, Liverpool John Moores University
Dr Deaglan Page, Queen's University, Belfast
Dr Julia Robertson, Buckinghamshire New University
Dr David Shaw, The Open University
Dr Michelle Tytherleigh, Department of Psychology, University of Chester
Dr Bob Williams, Durham University

Student reviewers:
Freya Chapman-Amey, Psychology student at Anglia Ruskin University
Tony Whalley, Psychology student at the University of Chester

We are grateful to the following for permission to reproduce copyright material:

Figures

Figure 4.1 from Mood-state-dependent retrieval: the effect of induced mood on memory reconsidered, *The Quarterly Journal of Experimental Psychology A: Human Experimental Psychology*, 50A (2), 290–317 (Kenealy, P. 1997), copyright © The Experimental

Acknowledgements

Psychology Society reprinted by permission of (Taylor & Francis Ltd, http://www.tandf.co.uk/journals) on behalf of The Experimental Psychology Society; Figure 4.3 from Context-dependent memory in two natural environments: on land and underwater, *British Journal of Psychology*, 66 (3), 325–331 (Godden, D.R. and Baddeley, A.D. 1975); Figure 4.4 from When does context influence recognition memory?, *British Journal of Psychology*, 71 (1), 99–104 (Godden, D.R. & Baddeley, A.D. 1980)

Tables

Table 10.1 adapted from *BPS Code of Ethics and Conduct: Guidance published by the Ethics Committee of the British Psychological Society*, British Psychological Society (2009)

Text

Extract on page 50 from The influence of in-store music on wine selections, *Journal of Applied Psychology*, 84 (2), 271–276 (1999), North, A.C., Hargreaves, D.J., & McKendrick, J. (1999). American Psychological Association. Reprinted with permission.

In some instances we have been unable to trace the owners of copyright material, and we would appreciate any information that would enable us to do so.

Introduction

Not only is psychology one of the fastest-growing subjects to study at university worldwide, it is also one of the most exciting and relevant subjects. Over the past decade the scope, breadth and importance of psychology have developed considerably. Important research work from as far afield as the UK, Europe, USA and Australia has demonstrated the exacting research base of the topic and how this can be applied to all manner of everyday issues and concerns. Being a student of psychology is an exciting experience – the study of mind and behaviour is a fascinating journey of discovery. Studying psychology at degree level brings with it new experiences, new skills and knowledge. As the Quality Assurance Agency (QAA) has stressed:

> psychology is distinctive in the rich and diverse range of attributes it develops – skills which are associated with the humanities (e.g. critical thinking and essay writing) and the sciences (hypotheses-testing and numeracy). (QAA, 2010, p. 5)

Recent evidence suggests that employers appreciate these skills and knowledge of psychology graduates, but in order to reach this pinnacle you need to develop your skills, further your knowledge and most of all successfully complete your degree to your maximum ability. The skills, knowledge and opportunities that you gain during your psychology degree will give you an edge in the employment field. The QAA stresses the high level of employment skills developed during a psychology degree:

> due to the wide range of generic skills, and the rigour with which they are taught, training in psychology is widely accepted as providing an excellent preparation for many careers. In addition to subject skills and knowledge, graduates also develop skills in communication, numeracy, teamwork, critical thinking, computing, independent learning and many others, all of which are highly valued by employers. (QAA, 2010, p. 2)

This book is part of the comprehensive new series, Psychology Express, that helps you achieve these aspirations. It is not a replacement for every single text, journal article, presentation and abstract you will read and review during the course of your degree programme. It is in no way a replacement for your lectures, seminars or additional reading. A top-rated assessment answer is likely to include considerable additional information and wider reading – and you are directed to some of these in this text. This revision guide is a conductor: directing you through the maze of your degree by providing an overview of your course, helping you formulate your ideas and directing your reading.

Each book within Psychology Express presents a summary coverage of the key concepts, theories and research in the field, within an explicit framework of revision. The focus throughout all of the books in the series will be on how you should approach and consider your topics in relation to assessment and exams. Various features have been included to help you build up your skills and knowledge, ready for your assessments. More details of the features can be found in the guided tour for this book on page xii.

By reading and engaging with this book, you will develop your skills and knowledge base and in this way you should excel in your studies and your associated assessments.

Psychology Express: Research Methods in Psychology is divided into 11 chapters and your course has probably been divided up into similar sections. However, we, the series authors and editor, must stress a key point: do not let the purchase, reading and engagement with the material in this text restrict your reading or your thinking. In psychology, you need to be aware of the wider literature and how it interrelates and how authors and thinkers have criticised and developed the arguments of others. So even if an essay asks you about one particular topic, you need to draw on similar issues raised in other areas of psychology. There are, of course, some similar themes that run throughout the material covered in this text, but you can learn from the other areas of psychology covered in the other texts in this series as well as from material presented elsewhere.

We hope you enjoy this text and the others in the Psychology Express series, which cover the complete knowledge base of psychology:

- *Biological Psychology* (Emma Preece): covering the biological basis of behaviour, hormones and behaviour, sleeping and dreaming, and psychological abnormalities.

- *Cognitive Psychology* (Jonathan Ling and Jonathan Catling): including key material on perception, learning, memory, thinking and language.

- *Developmental Psychology* (Penney Upton): from pre-natal development through to old age, the development of individuals is considered. Childhood, adolescence and lifespan development are all covered.

- *Personality and Individual Differences* (Terry Butler): normal and abnormal personality, psychological testing, intelligence, emotion and motivation are all covered in this book.

- *Social Psychology* (Jenny Mercer and Debbie Clayton): covering all the key topics in Social Psychology including attributions, attitudes, group relations, close relationships and critical social psychology.

- *Statistics in Psychology* (Catherine Steele, Holly Andrews and Dominic Upton): an overview of data analysis related to psychology is presented along with why we need statistics in psychology. Descriptive and inferential statistics and both parametric and non-parametric analysis are included.

- *Research Methods in Psychology* (Steve Jones and Mark Forshaw): research design, experimental methods, discussion of qualitative and quantitative methods and ethics are all presented in this text.

- *Conceptual and Historical Issues in Psychology* (Brian M. Hughes): the foundations of psychology and its development from a mere interest into a scientific discipline. The key conceptual issues of current-day psychology are also presented.

This book, and the other companion volumes in this series, should cover all your study needs (there will also be further guidance on the website). It will, obviously, need to be supplemented with further reading and this text directs you towards suitable sources. Hopefully, quite a bit of what you read here you will already have come across and the text will act as a jolt to set your mind at rest – you do know the material in depth. Overall, we hope that you find this book useful and informative as a guide for both your study now and in your future as a successful psychology graduate.

> **Revision note**
>
> - *Use evidence based on your reading, not on anecdotes or your 'common sense'.*
> - *Show the examiner you know your material in depth – use your additional reading wisely.*
> - *Remember to draw on a number of different sources: there is rarely one 'correct' answer to any psychological problem.*
> - *Base your conclusions on research-based evidence.*

> Explore the accompanying website at www.pearsoned.co.uk/psychologyexpress
> → Prepare more effectively for exams and assignments using the answer guidelines for questions from this chapter.
> → Test your knowledge using multiple choice questions and flashcards.
> → Improve your essay skills by exploring the You be the marker exercises.

Guided tour

→ Understand key concepts quickly

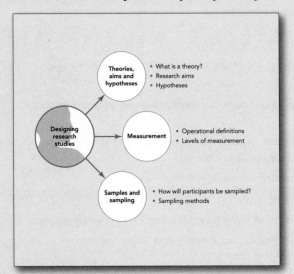

Start to plan your revision using the **Topic maps**.

Grasp **Key terms** quickly using the handy definitions. Use the flashcards online to test yourself.

Key term

Students often misunderstand the meaning of the term **rationale**, particularly when asked to write a rationale in the introduction to a research report. For the researcher, a rationale is much more than just a description of studies that have been undertaken previously; it is an integrated account of how those studies influenced the researcher's thinking when designing the research study. Why investigate a particular area in a certain way? What will it achieve? These are key elements in understanding what 'rationale' means.

→ Revise effectively

KEY STUDY

Dreams and eating disorders

Roger Knudson's case study of a woman with anorexia and her dreams is an interesting window on case study method in a therapeutic context and in the use of dreams to unveil concerns. Stephanie was battling with anorexia nervosa, but had given up with her therapist because the therapist was very insistent that Stephanie should be seeking hospital help. At the time of the dream that Stephanie had, she was so underweight that her life was actually at risk (which could explain the therapist's concern).

Stephanie dreamt that her room had a wall missing and her father was dressed very oddly to go to work. There was a monster in her swimming pool, which she could see from the hole in her bedroom wall. The monster jumped up from the pool to her room. She was forced to remain silent, trying not to be seen by the monster, and knowing her life was in danger. She realises that she has to deal with the monster and to look at it. She turns towards it and wakes up.

She went back to the therapist at this point, but the therapist offered the obvious interpretation (which of course could well be true) and again was keen to have Stephanie go to hospital. She rejected this once more.

Knudson discusses the various stances that have been taken on dreams and their interpretation, pointing out that dreams are not necessarily representations of reality and are not necessarily in a logical order. Therefore, his view is that the dream must be

Quickly remind yourself of the **Key studies** using the special boxes in the text.

Test your knowledge

1.5 What is the difference between deductive and inductive reasoning and how are they applied to the research process in psychology?

1.6 Explain why hypotheses or theories can never be 'proven' to be correct.

Answers to these questions can be found on the companion website at: www.pearsoned.co.uk/psychologyexpress

Prepare for upcoming exams and tests using the **Test your knowledge** and **Sample question** features.

Answer guidelines

 Sample question Essay

Using examples, show how single-case research can be experimental.

Approaching the question

Firstly, look carefully at the question and work out what is being asked for. The question asks only about single-case research, but that could include single-case series designs. It could also, theoretically, include case studies, which are not 'designs' but are a form of research, albeit not experimental. Examples are asked for. You'll also need to think about what 'experimental' means.

Important points to include

● Start with a paragraph alerting the reader to what you are going to discuss. This also tells them that you know what the question is about! Operationalise your definition of single-case research, showing what you wish to include in that definition and what you have decided does not fit.

Compare your responses with the **Answer guidelines** in the text and on the website.

→ Make your answers stand out

Use the **Critical focus** boxes to impress your examiner with your deep and critical understanding.

CRITICAL FOCUS

Participant observation

Participant observation is a specific type of observation that very few psychologists use, but that has been a mainstay of some of the most famous studies in sociology. Exactly as it sounds, participant observation is an unstructured method that requires the researcher to participate in the behaviour being observed. It is rather like working 'under cover', as the police or journalists often do. You join a group of people and do what they do, in order to discover what life is like for them. As you would imagine, this is an exciting and fascinating way to study behaviour and you can find things out that otherwise would remain hidden, but it is heavily flawed and unethical, so is seldom used any more. Covert participant observation is unethical because the people do not know that they are being studied and they do not know your true identity as a researcher.

Make your answer stand out

Your answer will stand out if you show that you have read around some of the issues and have a deeper understanding than just being able to supply accurate definitions and examples. The introduction of ecological validity to your answer, along with an understanding that it encapsulates much more than 'realism' would demonstrate a sophisticated level of understanding. Generally, take the opportunity to introduce discussion of replicability and generalisability and how they relate to reliability and validity. Take Professor Totoro and Dr Catbus further down the road and consider how they might be able to use their scales (if reliable and valid) and how they would be generalisable to different times, contexts and participant samples.

Go into the exam with confidence using the handy tips to **make your answer stand out**.

Guided tour of the companion website

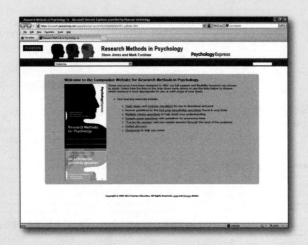

→ Understand key concepts quickly

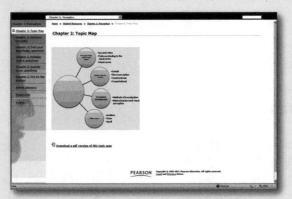

Printable versions of the **Topic maps** give an overview of the subject and help you plan your revision.

Test yourself on key definitions with the online **Flashcards**.

→ Revise effectively

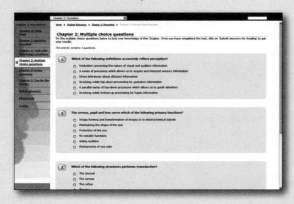

Check your understanding and practise for exams with the **Multiple choice questions**.

→ Make your answers stand out

Evaluate sample exam answers in the **You be the marker** exercises and understand how and why an examiner awards marks.

Put your skills into practice with the **Sample exam questions**, then check your answers with the guidelines.

All this and more can be found at
www.pearsoned.co.uk/psychologyexpress

Research in psychology

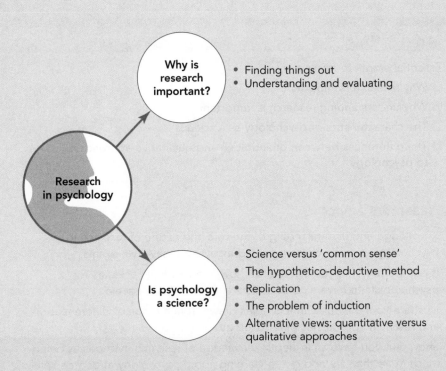

Why is research important?
- Finding things out
- Understanding and evaluating

Research in psychology

Is psychology a science?
- Science versus 'common sense'
- The hypothetico-deductive method
- Replication
- The problem of induction
- Alternative views: quantitative versus qualitative approaches

A printable version of this topic map is available from
www.pearsoned.co.uk/psychologyexpress

Introduction

You will need to understand why research is important in psychology and, crucially, appreciate why knowing about different approaches to research is central to developing the skills and knowledge expected of a psychology graduate. You will need to be able to explain how and why research and research methods are not separate from the issues and topics that are covered in the 'core areas' such as social psychology, developmental psychology or cognitive psychology. It is important that you do not view research methods in psychology as an entirely separate subject that is isolated from your understanding of any other aspect of the discipline. When studying research methods, it can be easy to focus on the detail and lose sight of the 'bigger picture' – that is, how the development of psychology is built entirely on questioning, investigation, analysis and evaluation.

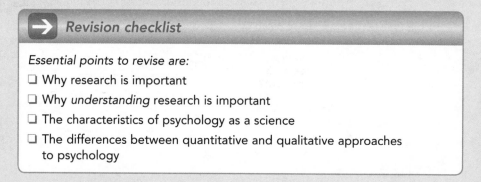

→ *Revision checklist*

Essential points to revise are:
- ❏ Why research is important
- ❏ Why *understanding* research is important
- ❏ The characteristics of psychology as a science
- ❏ The differences between quantitative and qualitative approaches to psychology

Assessment advice

- Knowledge and understanding of the role and nature of research in psychology are often assessed using essays or essay-style exams.
- It is important that you can explain how and why it is necessary for psychologists to have a good understanding of these issues.
- Illustrate your answer with examples drawn from a range of different areas and research approaches of psychology.
- Show that you have an in-depth knowledge of research methods as being much more than an 'add on' to learning about psychology at degree level.

Sample question

Could you answer this question? Below is a typical essay question that could arise on this topic.

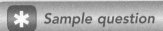

Sample question *Essay*

Discuss whether psychological research is scientific.

Guidelines on answering this question are included at the end of this chapter, whilst further guidance on tackling other exam questions can be found on the companion website at: **www.pearsoned.co.uk/psychologyexpress**

Why is research important?

There are two main, interrelated reasons why research and understanding research methods are important. The first is the most obvious: finding things out.

Finding things out

Research forms the bedrock of modern psychology. Textbooks in all areas of psychology (e.g. developmental, social or cognitive psychology) are filled with summaries and explanations of theories and models. There are descriptions of studies and findings and interpretations of what they might mean. All of these ideas and theories exist only because psychologists have conducted research. Without this, psychology as a subject would simply have no content and would consist entirely of empty speculation and unsubstantiated 'common sense'. Psychology is an empirical discipline. This means that ideas in psychology are developed by collecting evidence from the world around us, by using various methods, including observation and experiments. These are the processes by which psychological knowledge develops and how we have something called 'psychology' to learn about.

Understanding and evaluating

In addition to conducting research to develop psychological knowledge and acquire an understanding of human behaviour, having a shared knowledge of research methods is crucial to allow us to understand and evaluate research findings. This evaluation and close examination of the methods used in psychological research enables us to draw our own conclusions about the evidence and how convincing it is. The evidence collected from a well-designed and carefully controlled study will carry much more weight than anecdotal evidence collected from, for example, a very small unrepresentative sample. While this point may seem obvious, the definition of what is 'well designed' or 'carefully controlled' can be judged only by someone who has an understanding of the ins-and-outs of research methods in psychology and the principles of good design. This is another major reason why everyone engaged in the study or practice of psychology needs to have a full understanding and appreciation of research methods in psychology.

Practitioners of psychology, including those involved in such areas as health, occupational, clinical and forensic psychology, are usually involved in directly advising and helping individuals and organisations to solve problems, operate more effectively and so on. Their knowledge and understanding of what type of intervention is likely to be effective in a particular situation will be based on the research evidence that suggests this. An ability to evaluate studies that claim to demonstrate the utility of a specific approach is, therefore, essential for the psychology practitioner.

Evaluating research and identifying its strengths, weaknesses and aspects that merit further investigation help the researcher to take the next steps in 'finding things out'. This process of research and evaluation is essential for psychology to develop as a science. Otherwise, we would be trapped in a loop of forever repeating the same mistakes and making the same 'discoveries' over and over again. We must appreciate and evaluate what has gone before in order to progress.

Test your knowledge

1.1 Why is research important to psychology?

1.2 Why must undergraduate psychology students learn about research methods?

Answers to these questions can be found on the companion website at: **www.pearsoned.co.uk/psychologyexpress**

Is psychology a science?

As already mentioned, the process of research and evaluation is fundamental to the development of psychology as a 'science'. However, whilst people generally agree that disciplines such as biology, physics and astronomy are 'sciences', it is by no means universally accepted that psychology *is* a 'science' or, indeed, that the areas that should form the central interest for psychology lend themselves to scientific study.

Science versus 'common sense'

People who have not studied psychology sometimes argue that psychological research findings are 'obvious' or that 'everybody knows that'. This is because psychology is involved in studying human behaviour, and people tend to think that they already know everything they need to about this from their own personal experiences.

Science, however, involves a particular way of thinking about and investigating the world that differentiates it from 'everyday knowledge' and common sense. The key differences between scientific and non-scientific thinking are shown in Figure 1.1.

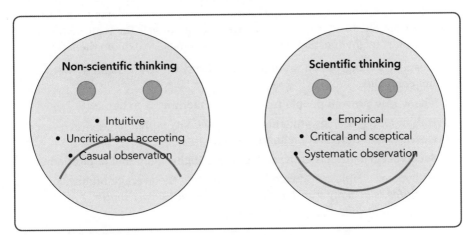

Figure 1.1 **Non-scientific versus scientific thinking**

A scientific approach relies on the collection of empirical data (that is, the evidence is collected by making systematic observations in the world, and not merely through theorising and conjecture). This is relatively uncontroversial in psychology; most psychologists agree that we can learn about human behaviour only by directly studying it. That is, however, where any semblance of consensus ends. Science is characterised by careful measurement and control, and by the development of theories and testing of hypotheses. The vast majority of research in psychology has been, and continues to be, of this type. However, some psychologists do not agree that human behaviour should be investigated using these methods, and argue that human experience is far too complex to be reduced to the levels of explanation employed within these types of investigation.

The fact remains, however, that the vast majority of psychological research that has been undertaken to date has been built upon scientific principles and, particularly, the application of the 'hypothetico-deductive method', which is often referred to simply as 'the scientific method'.

Further reading	Science versus common sense	
Topic	_Key reading_
An overview of theory construction, including the scientific method	Marx, M. H. (1963). The general nature of theory construction. In M. H. Marx (Ed.), _Theories in contemporary psychology_ (pp. 4-46). New York: Macmillan.

Sample question | *Assessment*

On the basis of their everyday casual observations, experiences and knowledge, here are some 'facts' and reported research findings that the unscientific, uncritical person may accept at face value as being both correct and informative. In each case, give a brief account of how the critical scientific psychologist might question the basis of each of these to explore them further.

1 Heat causes aggression, so that explains why there are so many wars in hot countries.

2 The way to prevent people from doing something is to ban it.

3 Half of all psychology students leave university with a degree classification that is worse than average.

4 An 8-year-old girl has an IQ of 150. That's higher than that of most adults!

5 Millions of people worldwide have more than the average number of legs (*this is actually true, but explain why it isn't surprising!*)

6 We use only 10 per cent of our brains.

The hypothetico-deductive method

As the predominant approach in psychological research, an understanding of this method is essential in appreciating and evaluating research in psychology and the conclusions to be drawn from it. The general principles are that theories are evaluated through the generation and testing of specific predictions about what will happen under particular conditions. These specific predictions are what we refer to as 'hypotheses'. The approach is summarised in Figure 1.2.

One interesting feature to note and remember about this process is that it doesn't have an end! On the left-hand side of the diagram, the arrow outlined with dotted lines suggests that when results support the hypothesis, further hypotheses should be developed to test the theory further. Of course, conducting a study and finding that the hypothesis is supported is very important, and the published results of that study would advance knowledge of the subject. It also would not be necessary for the *same* researcher to follow the path indicated by the dotted-line arrow; that could be the work of others. This further, follow-up work indicates two very important features of scientific enquiry and the hypothetico-deductive method: 'replication' and 'the problem of induction'.

Replication

A research finding is only really of value if it can be replicated. Basically, if a theory and the hypotheses derived from it are correct, then the same findings should emerge if the study is repeated. It is always possible that any single set of results might be due to a chance occurrence, so in order for firm conclusions to be drawn, it is necessary for the effect to be replicated. This is another

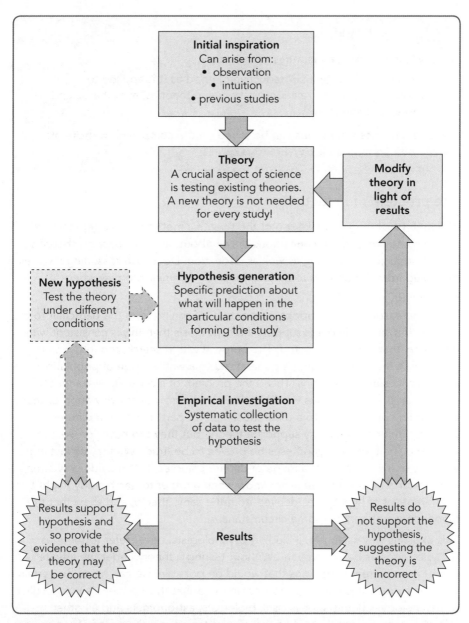

Figure 1.2 The hypothetico-deductive method

reason why researchers in psychology adopt scientific approaches, and why it is vital that psychologists have a shared understanding of research and research methods. This may also be why your lecturer in research methods continually emphasises the need to write clear reports of your research practicals: if the report isn't clear, the study will not be replicable, and the scientific process runs into a dead-end!

The problem of induction

Although psychologists make use of the scientific method, the acceptance of research findings and the conclusions drawn about how they support theories involve 'inductive' reasoning as well as deduction. Deductive reasoning involves reasoning from the general to the particular, and comes into play when developing hypotheses.

Inductive reasoning is the opposite; it entails reasoning from the particular to the general. If a study's findings support the hypothesis then this is consistent with the theory that was being tested. The purpose with research, though, is to try to establish theories that can be generalised to a whole range of populations, circumstances and conditions. This is the problem of induction: we cannot be certain that the same results would be found tomorrow or the day after, or that they would apply equally to a different sample of participants in a different location. Empirical data may support a theory, but they can never *prove* it to be correct, neither can hypotheses be *proven* to be 'true'. We may collect huge amounts of evidence, from a range of different studies, that provide very strong support for a theory, but we never know when another research study might test a different set of hypotheses derived from the same theory, and show that the theory does not apply in some circumstances.

This explains why scientists, including psychologists, never refer to theories or hypotheses as being 'proven'. Without testing a theory under the infinite number of different conditions that would be possible, we can never be *certain* that it is correct. It is important to bear in mind that this problem is not peculiar to psychology. Chemists, physicists, biologists, astronomers and all other scientists must accept that, while the current theories in their area of expertise may be supported by huge amounts of strong evidence, there is always the possibility that the next research study may produce evidence to suggest the theory is not correct or does not apply in all conditions and, therefore, needs to be modified.

Further reading **Psychology as science**

Topic	Key reading
Why psychology is scientific	Mukunda, K. V. (1997). Is psychology a science? *Resonance, 2*(11), 59–66.
Why psychology is (and isn't!) scientific	Uttal, W. R. (2007). *The immeasurable mind: The real science of psychology.* Amherst, NY: Prometheus Books.

Test your knowledge

1.5 What is the difference between deductive and inductive reasoning and how are they applied to the research process in psychology?

1.6 Explain why hypotheses or theories can never be 'proven' to be correct.

Answers to these questions can be found on the companion website at:
www.pearsoned.co.uk/psychologyexpress

CRITICAL FOCUS

Karl Popper and falsifiability

Popper (1959) argued that scientific investigation should not be about attempting to provide evidence to *support* theories, but should involve striving to falsify theories by showing them to be wrong. While we cannot prove that theories are true, we can demonstrate when a theory is incorrect. Popper's view was that science did not actually have problems with inductive reasoning, because that was not the primary method that was, or should be, employed anyway! He argued that scientists should actively attempt to collect data that falsify a theory. Repeated failures to falsify a theory mean that that theory can be accepted, at least for the time being. In other words, science progresses, not through asserting theories to be universally true, but by accepting when there is no apparent reason for believing a theory to be false.

Source: Popper, K. (1959) *The logic of scientific discovery*. New York: Basic Books.

? Sample question   *Assessment*

1 Do you think that Popper's argument resolves the problem of induction?

2 Is this thinking consistent with the hypothetico-deductive method?

3 Psychology often offers alternative explanations of the same observed phenomena. How do Popper's ideas help us to evaluate which is the best theory?

4 How can falsifying a theory help to develop an alternative explanation?

Alternative views: quantitative versus qualitative approaches

The distinction between quantitative and qualitative approaches can be, broadly, thought of as 'measurement' versus 'meaning'. Quantitative approaches, as the name suggests, emphasise the measurement and quantification of human behaviour whereas qualitative approaches are more concerned with exploring the ways in which individuals think about, talk about and interpret and understand the world around them.

It is important to appreciate that there are fundamental differences between these two types of approach in terms of the types of questions that they ask (more about this in the next chapter), the methods that they employ and the conclusions that they aim to produce (covered in later chapters). Qualitative studies are not designed to test hypotheses derived from theories. The other key differences between quantitative and qualitative approaches are summarised in Table 1.1.

Table 1.1 Quantitative versus qualitative methods

Quantitative	Qualitative
Emphasises precise measurement	Emphasises the exploration of meaning
Uses carefully controlled studies	Employs open-ended and exploratory studies
Aims to identify causal relationships between variables and to develop predictive models	Aims to offer in-depth description and interpretation of how individuals understand the world
Attempts to isolate individual variables as explanatory factors	Argues that human experience is complex and cannot be reduced to simple explanations
Not concerned with individual subjective experience	Values and emphasises subjective experiences of individuals
Researcher is objective and makes every effort not to influence or contaminate the study or its results	Researcher is an integral part of the research process and reflects on their own contribution and influence on the study and its findings
Relies on replication of findings to consolidate and generalise conclusions	Each study has its own intrinsic value, and the emphasis on subjectivity means that replication is not an appropriate concept
Primary methods include experiments, questionnaires and quantifiable observational studies	Primary methods include interviews with individuals or groups, text analysis and descriptive observational studies

The distinction between 'quantitative' and 'qualitative' is not as straightforward as it may seem. It is important to understand that 'qualitative' does not refer to a single method but, rather, a way of conceptualising research in ways that are very different from the methods of quantitative approaches. There are several different types of qualitative approach, and there can be almost as much disagreement between proponents of these different methods as between qualitative and quantitative researchers. These issues will be covered in a later chapter.

Further reading Qualitative methods and science	
Topic	Key reading
Argues that qualitative research in psychology is scientific	Harré, R. (2004). Staking our claim for qualitative psychology as science. *Qualitative Research in Psychology, 1*(1), 3–14.

Chapter summary – pulling it all together

→ Can you tick all the points from the revision checklist at the beginning of this chapter?

→ Attempt the sample question from the beginning of this chapter using the answer guidelines below.

→ Go to the companion website at www.pearsoned.co.uk/psychologyexpress to access more revision support online, including interactive quizzes, flashcards, You be the marker exercises as well as answer guidance for the Test your knowledge and Sample questions from this chapter.

Answer guidelines

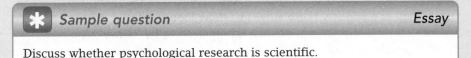

✱ *Sample question*   *Essay*

Discuss whether psychological research is scientific.

Approaching the question

The question asks you to discuss whether psychology is a 'science'. The general approach to take is a critical one that demonstrates a broad understanding of the issues. You will need to show that you have considered all of the factors that impact on the definition of 'scientific' research.

Important points to include

- A starting point may be to discuss the general principles and ways of thinking that characterise science and differentiate it from everyday 'common-sense' ideas. Relate this directly to psychology, so use examples drawn from the types of topic areas that psychologists investigate. The more specific detail will involve a discussion of the hypothetico-deductive method and its application in psychology. The psychological literature abounds with potential examples, so you should easily be able to draw in illustrative examples from the 'core' areas of psychology that you have studied. An important point to remember is that, if psychology is a science, then it also shares the same weaknesses that other sciences do, so you can draw in a discussion of induction and Popper's principle of falsifiability. Introduce the idea that there are different ways of researching psychology, and that qualitative methods are more interested in 'meaning' rather than 'measuring'. These approaches do not fit the traditional notion of 'science' but may still offer fruitful findings and insights.

● Finally, don't forget that the advancement of knowledge in any scientific subject relies on a shared understanding between its researchers and practitioners, which is why it is crucial that psychology students understand research methods and are able to evaluate research evidence. This point may also please your research methods tutor and show that you appreciate their efforts!

Make your answer stand out

It is easy to focus entirely on the traditional notion of 'science' as characterised by the scientific method and the testing of hypotheses. Particularly, if you want to offer a sophisticated and complex set of arguments, you can make your answer stand out by challenging the notion that quantitative research in psychology is scientific, but qualitative research is not. Rom Harré's (2004) discussion opens up a whole range of issues in this area as he argues that qualitative approaches in psychology satisfy the criteria for 'science' better than quantitative methods! In addition to challenging the simple distinction between quantitative and qualitative methods, you might wonder what this tells us about the status of 'science'. Rather than challenge the notion of psychology as a science, Harré strives to show that qualitative research is 'science'. A discussion of why science is perceived to be 'better' than non-scientific methods would really help your answer to stand out.

Finally, remember to draw in examples from various areas of psychology, as this will help you to show that you understand the issues and, crucially, that you are aware how knowing about research in psychology is essential to evaluate and critique research findings across the whole discipline.

Explore the accompanying website at www.pearsoned.co.uk/psychologyexpress
→ Prepare more effectively for exams and assignments using the answer guidelines for questions from this chapter.
→ Test your knowledge using multiple choice questions and flashcards.
→ Improve your essay skills by exploring the You be the marker exercises.

Notes

Notes

2

Designing research studies

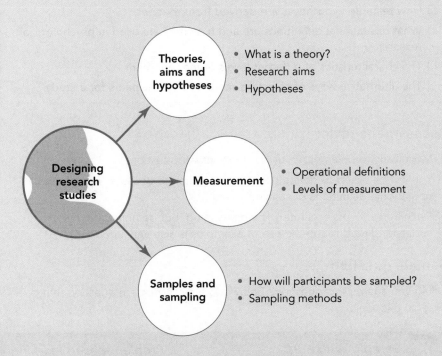

- Theories, aims and hypotheses
  - What is a theory?
  - Research aims
  - Hypotheses

- Designing research studies

- Measurement
  - Operational definitions
  - Levels of measurement

- Samples and sampling
  - How will participants be sampled?
  - Sampling methods

A printable version of this topic map is available from
www.pearsoned.co.uk/psychologyexpress

Introduction

The links between theories, hypotheses, measures and samples are central to designing research studies in psychology. You will need to be able to define these concepts accurately and to demonstrate that you understand how to use and apply them to examples of psychological research studies. As with many of the concepts in research methods in psychology, it is this ability to apply the principles to examples from research, and to show that you can determine, for instance, whether hypotheses are appropriate and testable, that is important.

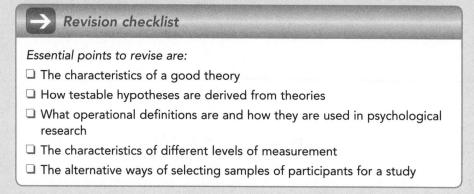

→ Revision checklist

Essential points to revise are:
- ❏ The characteristics of a good theory
- ❏ How testable hypotheses are derived from theories
- ❏ What operational definitions are and how they are used in psychological research
- ❏ The characteristics of different levels of measurement
- ❏ The alternative ways of selecting samples of participants for a study

Assessment advice

- Most likely to be assessed using short-answer questions.
- You will be asked to define concepts, or generate or assess hypotheses, operational definitions or sampling methods.
- Defining concepts accurately is a good thing, but demonstrating your understanding through the use of examples is also very important.

Sample question

Could you answer this question? Below is a typical problem question that could arise on this topic.

 ✳ Sample question   *Problem-based learning*

The following is based on Hurlbert, A. C., & Ling, Y. (2007). Biological components of sex differences in color preference. *Current Biology*, 17(16), R623–R65.

Hurlbert and Ling (2007) tested 28 British females, 25 British males, 18 Chinese females and 19 Chinese males, aged 20–26, on a colour-preference task. The task involved selecting which of two colours they preferred as the colours appeared in pairs on a computer screen. Participants performed the task on two occasions, two weeks apart.

British female participants showed a preference for reddish-purple colours, and British males showed a preference for blue-green, albeit with a weaker preference than that shown by females. Chinese participants of both sexes showed a preference for reddish colours.

The preferences of female participants remained more stable across the two-week period than the preferences of the male participants.

Hurlbert and Ling 'speculate that this sex difference arose from sex-specific functional specializations in the evolutionary division of labor. The hunter-gatherer theory proposes that female brains should be specialized for gathering-related tasks' and have 'evolved to facilitate the identification of ripe, yellow fruit or edible red leaves embedded in green foliage'. They also offer an alternative explanation, which is that females 'need to discriminate subtle changes in skin color due to emotional states and social-sexual signals; again, females may have honed these adaptations for their roles as care-givers and "empathizers"'.

1 Evaluate the explanations offered by Hurlbert and Ling for their findings.

2 Develop research hypotheses from the two explanations, and devise studies to test those hypotheses. What elements must be considered in designing the studies, and how would you address them?

Guidelines on answering this question are included at the end of this chapter, whilst further guidance on tackling other exam questions can be found on the companion website at: **www.pearsoned.co.uk/psychologyexpress**

Theories, aims and hypotheses

What is a theory?

A theory is a logically organised set of claims or statements that serves to explain observed phenomena and the relationships between them. The three main purposes of theories are to describe, explain and predict, as explained in Figure 2.1.

Theories may be simple, short and general (e.g. sunshine is a cause of happiness) or they may be much more lengthy, involved and complex, as they may be accounting for a series of complicated relationships between concepts; think, for example, of Piaget's Theory of Child Development. This consists of an extensive set of ideas and concepts, intended to provide an account of the staged development of children's cognitive abilities. There are lots of other theories in psychology that set out lengthy explanations of the causes of various phenomena in human behaviour.

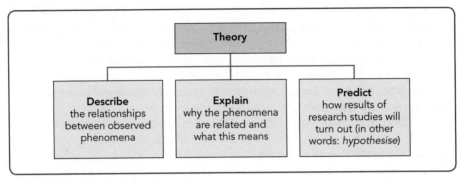

Figure 2.1 Three purposes of a theory

Theories allow us to organise our research findings and to guide further research. A theory is only of scientific value if it can be tested and refuted. The characteristics of good scientific theories are as shown in Figure 2.2.

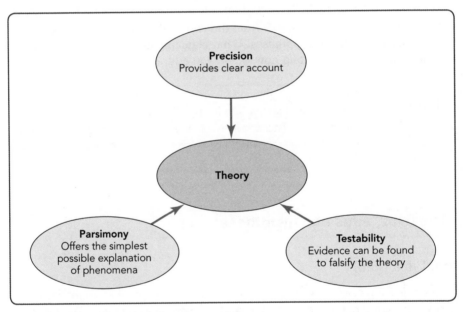

Figure 2.2 Three characteristics of a good theory

Further reading	Theory in psychology
Topic	*Key reading*
Discusses the application of scientific principles to research in social psychology	Trope, Y. (2004). Theory in social psychology: Seeing the forest and the trees. *Personality & Social Psychology Review, 8*(2), 193–200.
Discussion of what constitutes a good theory in psychology	Klein, K., & Zedeck, S. (2004). Theory in applied psychology: Lessons (re)learned. *Journal of Applied Psychology, 89*(6), 931–933.

Test your knowledge

2.1 What are the key characteristics of a good theory?

2.2 What does a theory allow us to do?

Answers to these questions can be found on the companion website at:
www.pearsoned.co.uk/psychologyexpress

Research aims

When designing a research study, the researcher must think very carefully about the aims of the study. What is it that the researcher hopes to achieve through conducting the study? This is closely related to the concept of a *rationale*; the researcher must be clear not only about what they hope to achieve, but also be able to be offer a detailed account of *why* they have developed those aims and what their ideas are based on. Other key questions that researchers need to address include the extent to which psychological knowledge could be advanced by the study and why anyone would be interested in the results. In other words, is there any point finding these things out? The developed aims and rationale for the study lead, in turn, to the development and statement of hypotheses.

Key term

Students often misunderstand the meaning of the term **rationale**, particularly when asked to write a rationale in the introduction to a research report. For the researcher, a rationale is much more than just a description of studies that have been undertaken previously; it is an integrated account of how those studies influenced the researcher's thinking when designing the research study. Why investigate a particular area in a certain way? What will it achieve? These are key elements in understanding what 'rationale' means.

Hypotheses

A theory can often lead to the development of several different hypotheses, and the more complex the theory, the more aspects there will be that require testing. The hypothesis is, basically, a tentative explanation of the relationships between variables. In practice this most often translates into a prediction about how the results of a study will turn out. It is important that the hypothesis for a study is as specific as possible so that it can be tested in a way that clearly and unambiguously allows the hypothesis to be accepted or rejected. Hypotheses may be directional (e.g. 'women will perform better than men on a verbal reasoning task') or non-directional (e.g. 'there will be a difference between the performance of women and men on a verbal reasoning task'). If previous research findings and the theory to be tested suggest a directional relationship between phenomena, then a directional hypothesis should be used. It can be tempting to hedge one's bets and try to maximise the possibility of being 'right' by using a non-directional hypothesis where a directional hypothesis is indicated, but this is very bad practice, is unscientific and should be avoided.

When set within the context of statistical testing, directional and non-directional hypotheses are referred to as 'one-tailed' and 'two-tailed', respectively.

Testability

In order to be testable, an hypothesis must be clear, precise and unambiguous. There are three main problems that may arise in defining the hypotheses for a study. These are inadequate definition of concepts, circularity and appealing to forces beyond those recognised by science. Figure 2.3 briefly explains these problems.

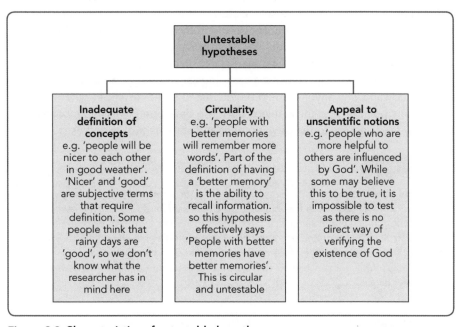

Figure 2.3 Characteristics of untestable hypotheses

Test your knowledge

2.3 What are the key characteristics of a good hypothesis?

2.4 What are the three main problems that may render hypotheses untestable?

2.5 For each of the following hypotheses, consider whether the hypothesis is testable or not and, if not, identify the problem that makes it untestable.

(a) God answers our prayers.

(b) Friendly people are more helpful than unfriendly people.

(c) Women have better memories than men.

(d) Love changes everything.

(e) If you want to find a fool in the countryside, you'll have to take one with you.

Answers to these questions can be found on the companion website at: www.pearsoned.co.uk/psychologyexpress

Correlational versus causal hypotheses

Theories in psychology can involve the correlations, or associations, between variables or can suggest the causal relationships between them. Consequently, research hypotheses and the studies designed to test them may be of a correlational or causal nature.

It is important to appreciate the problems that psychologists are faced with when trying to determine causal relationships between two variables and the care that must be taken when interpreting the relationships between two variables. There are three key conditions that must be met for the conclusion to be reached that one thing causes another. These are shown in Figure 2.4.

In psychology, the way in which researchers investigate the causal relationships between variables is through the use of carefully controlled experiments in which one variable is manipulated to see what effects it has on another variable. Note that, rather than talking about 'cause', researchers in psychology tend to refer to the 'effects' of one variable on another. It is also possible to draw inferences about causation from observational studies, but these lack the control and precision of experimental studies.

Correlational hypotheses can be tested in a number of ways, but the main principle is that various measures are taken simultaneously or, in any case, without actively manipulating anything. Note that just because correlational hypotheses do not state that A *causes* B, this does not mean that correlational hypotheses cannot be directional.

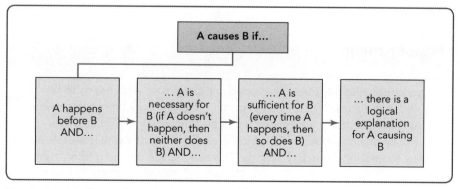

Figure 2.4 Conditions for determining causality

Key term

Correlation very specifically refers to a non-causal relationship between variables. Avoid using this term when what is being investigated is an effect that has been directly caused by manipulating a variable in an experimental study.

Further reading Causality

Topic	Key reading
Discusses the importance of causality and how it applies to operant conditioning	Ribes-Inesta, E. (1997). Causality and contingency: Some conceptual considerations. *Psychological Record*, *47*(4), 619.

Test your knowledge

2.6 What are the conditions for determining that one event causes another?

2.7 For each of the following, evaluate the conclusion about the causal link between the two events. Does one cause the other or might both be caused by something else?

(a) The more firefighters there are at a fire, the bigger the fire. Therefore, firefighters cause the fire.

(b) Taller children are better at reading. Therefore, growing taller causes reading to improve.

(c) People who watch violent movies are more aggressive than people who don't. Therefore, watching violent movies causes aggression.

(d) More people have umbrellas when it rains. Therefore, having an umbrella causes it to rain.

Answers to these questions can be found on the companion website at: **www.pearsoned.co.uk/psychologyexpress**

Measurement

The hypothesis that has been developed will determine what needs to be measured in the study. There is an important distinction to be made between psychological constructs on the one hand, and the way in which they are measured on the other. A psychological construct is anything that we talk about and seek to understand in psychology. This can include anything from 'memory' or 'attention' through to 'intelligence', 'creativity', 'sexism', 'stress', 'anxiety' or even 'love'. These are 'constructs' because they are our ways of organising our understanding of human behaviour. Nobody has ever directly observed 'love'. What is directly observable is behaviour that may be indicative of 'love'. In order to conduct research and test hypotheses, researchers need to be able to define the constructs under investigation in terms of ways in which they can be measured. These are called 'operational definitions'.

Operational definitions

There are various ways in which psychological constructs can be operationally defined and measured. If we take the hypothesis that women have better verbal skills than men, there are any number of ways in which we can define what we mean by 'verbal skills' for the purposes of a study. We might define verbal skills in terms of the time it takes to solve a set of crossword clues, how many words could be generated from a particular category in a given time or how many unusual words can be correctly defined in a written test. We could also count how many times per minute each participant uses the words 'like', 'you know' or 'kinda thing' when engaged in a conversation or when asked to describe everyday objects and their uses (with higher levels of use representing lower levels of verbal ability). It is important to understand that operational definitions may change from study to study and that where differences arise between the results of different studies testing the same theory, the operational definitions employed within the studies may be a cause of the differences.

Operational definitions must be *valid*. It would make no sense to operationally define verbal ability as the number of dot-to-dot puzzles that can be completed in five minutes. There has to be a clear, unambiguous and explicit link between the measure and the psychological construct that it is supposed to be tapping into.

Key term

An **operational definition** involves defining a concept in terms of how it can be measured. It is the measurability that is the key element here.

Test your knowledge

2.8 Why are operational definitions so important in researching psychological constructs?

2.9 For each of the following, suggest an operational definition that could be employed in a research study (and do not just resort to answering 'Score on a questionnaire' for them all. Be more imaginative!).

(a) Reading speed

(b) Aggression

(c) Creativity

(d) Helpfulness

▶

> **2.10** Provide operational definitions that would make this hypothesis testable: 'If you want to find a fool in the countryside, you'll have to take one with you.'
>
> Answers to these questions can be found on the companion website at: **www.pearsoned.co.uk/psychologyexpress**

Levels of measurement

An important consideration when designing a study and operationally defining variables is the level of measurement that will be used in the study. There are four types of measurement scale: nominal (or categorical), ordinal, interval and ratio. It is easy to learn these labels as a list, but it is crucial to appreciate why researchers must understand the distinctions between different types of measurement scale. The level of measurement refers to the type of data that will be collected and determines how the results of the study can be analysed as well as what types of conclusions can be drawn from the findings. Effective research design involves planning ahead and thinking about these issues before beginning the data collection for a study. A failure to consider how the measurements will be taken and how they link to the study's aims and hypotheses may result in it being impossible to use the collected data to test the hypotheses. The distinctions between the different levels of measurement are, consequently, much more than an abstract set of concepts. For each level of measurement, the key points are:

- the characteristics of that type of measurement
- what the collected data do and do not allow the researcher to conclude
- using examples to demonstrate an understanding of these issues.

It is, perhaps, easiest to make sense of the different levels of measurement by starting at 'the top' and working 'downwards' in the order ratio, interval, ordinal, nominal.

Ratio data

Ratio data most closely resemble what most people would think of as 'measuring'. On a ratio scale, all of the points are arranged at equal intervals and there is a 'true zero'. In other words, zero on the scale corresponds with zero of the concept to be measured. If an object weighs zero kilograms, then it has no weight. If someone recalls zero words from a list, then they have zero memory (as operationally defined!). The existence of a true zero allows us to talk in terms of 'ratios' (hence the name). If Bert recalls 40 out of 100 words and Tom recalls 20, then we can conclude that Bert has recalled twice as many as Tom. The numerical values on the scale (e.g. 40 and 20) tell us not just that Bert has scored more highly than Tom, but what the relationship between the scores was. If Dave scored 0, then we could conclude that the distance on the scale from

Dave to Tom represents the same difference in performance as the distance from Tom to Bert.

In psychology, the two main commonly occurring types of ratio scale are number correct on a test and the time taken to complete a task. Time is a classic example of a ratio scale: the labels on the scale are all spaced at equal intervals (the distance from 11 to 12 seconds is the same as that from 45 to 46 seconds) and there is a true zero (zero seconds equates to taking no time, and it is not possible to have less than zero).

In practice, however, the benefits of being able to draw conclusions about the 'ratio' of one score to another are limited. Psychologists do not often discuss their research findings in these terms, so the 'true zero' of the ratio scale does not really offer much advantage over the type of measurement scale which does not have a true zero, but on which the points are spaced at equal intervals: the interval scale.

Interval data

On an interval scale, the data points are equally spaced so that we know the distance from 10 to 20, for example, represents the same increase in the concept being measured as the increase from 20 to 30. While this certainly holds true for concepts such as 'number correct on a test' or 'time', for other psychological constructs things are not always as clear-cut. Psychologists often make use of rating scales and questionnaires to measure concepts such as motivation, attitudes, anxiety, stress and so on. If, for example, participants are asked to rate how much they like cheese on a 1 to 10 scale with a higher score representing more liking, we cannot be sure that the difference in liking between scores of 9 and 10 is the same as that between 4 and 5. Psychologically, there may well be a bigger difference between a shift from 9 to 10 on this scale than from 4 to 5, as people may be reluctant to use the highest point. The same problem arises with all types of rating scale.

In practice, data derived from this type of rating scale (typically from questionnaire studies) are treated as though they are interval data, but it is important to be aware of the issues and to show that you do not routinely treat all types of data as interval data without careful consideration. It can be argued that standardised questionnaires that have been tested on a large sample of people and found to produce a normal distribution of scores can be treated as interval data. However, it does not necessarily follow that normal distributions represent scores collected on an interval scale.

Collecting data at the interval or ratio levels opens up the full range of statistical analyses to the researcher. When the data lie on an interval scale, it makes sense to talk about 'average' scores and conclusions can be drawn about how one group has performed on the test relative to others.

Where there is doubt about whether the data collected from a particular study should be treated as interval data, they should be considered to be ordinal.

Ordinal data

Measurement on an ordinal scale provides information about the ranked position of observations ('ordinal' refers to 'order'). On the 'cheese liking' scale, we can conclude that a higher score represents a greater liking for cheese (but not that the points on the scale are spaced at equal intervals). Ordinal scales provide information about the order of the data, but not of the spacing between them. If, for example, the results of race indicate that Dave came first, Martin was second and Eric third, this tells us about the order in which they finished, but nothing about the distances between them. This is an ordinal scale, as, for example, is the UK Singles Chart.

In psychology, ordinal data are most commonly produced by taking a numerical measure and then converting the scores into ordinal data for the purposes of analysis. The 'cheese liking' scale, for example, collects a series of scores ranging from 1 to 10. If we tested 20 people, we could convert their scores into ranks, so we end up with a list of the 20 participants in the order in which they like cheese. In other words, the actual scores that they gave us on the rating scale would disappear. This sometimes seems like an odd thing to do, but remember that there was nothing special about the ratings on the scale; the scale was not an interval scale, so there was nothing to be gained by knowing the actual score beyond being able to identify which participants liked cheese more than others.

With ordinal data, care must be taken with summarising and interpreting the scores. If, as described, the data are not interval, then calculating a mean score using the original data might not be informative. It may be more useful to know the mean *ranked score* rather than the mean of the raw data.

Nominal (or categorical) data

As the name implies, the collection of this type of data involves naming or categorising. Sometimes, the design of the study will determine this as the most appropriate way of collecting the data. For example, if a researcher hypothesises that more female students than male students spend time working in the library, this can be achieved by walking through the library and categorising each person working in there as 'male' or 'female'. This would then produce a total number (or frequency) for each, which would allow the researcher to test the hypothesis.

The key characteristic of this type of measurement is that each observation fits into a category. There is no way of distinguishing between any two members of the same category. For example, if participants are asked whether they like cheese or not, the researcher would end up with a total number for each of the two categories. If Sam and Bert both like cheese this does not allow us to distinguish between them in terms of how much they like it. It might be that Sam really loves cheese but Bert only likes it a little bit.

Categorical data do not lend themselves to meaningful calculations of mean scores. For example, if the researcher found 20 females and 25 males in the library, it would be possible to 'score' each female as 1 and each male as 2, and conclude that the mean gender of the students in the library was 1.56.

However, while this is possible, it is also nonsensical. Categorical data cannot be treated in this way, and it is the potential for mishandling data in this way that underpins the need to understand different levels of measurement.

Further reading **Measurement**	
Topic	*Key reading*
The issues around how psychology defines 'measurement' and how this relates to scientific principles (a bit complicated in places, but worth a read!)	Michell, J. (1997). Quantitative science and the definition of measurement in psychology. *British Journal of Psychology*, 88(3), 355–383.
Counter-arguments to Michell's ideas (a good example of an academic debate appearing in a single volume of a journal)	Kline, P. (1997). Commentary on Michell, quantitative science and the definition of measurement in psychology. *British Journal of Psychology*, 88(3), 385.
	Laming, D. (1997). A critique of a measurement-theoretic critique: Commentary on Michell, quantitative science and the definition of measurement in psychology. *British Journal of Psychology*, 88(3), 389.
	Lovie, A. (1997). Commentary on Michell, quantitative science and the definition of measurement in psychology. *British Journal of Psychology*, 88(3), 393.
	Luce, R. (1997). Quantification and symmetry: Commentary on Michell, quantitative science and definition of measurement in psychology. *British Journal of Psychology*, 88(3), 395–398.
	Morgan, M. (1997). Measurement in psychology: Commentary on Michell's quantitative science and the definition of measurement in psychology. *British Journal of Psychology*, 88(3), 399.
Michell's reply to the criticisms	Michell, J. (1997). Reply to Kline, Laming, Lovie, Luce, and Morgan. *British Journal of Psychology*, 88(3), 401.

Test your knowledge

2.11 Why do researchers need to know about levels of measurement?

2.12 The following results are from a study investigating the time, in seconds, that it took ten participants to spot the difference between two pictures. How can these results be converted into ordinal and nominal data?

12, 15, 5, 7, 4, 13, 11, 8, 10, 6

Answers to these questions can be found on the companion website at: **www.pearsoned.co.uk/psychologyexpress**

Samples and sampling

Research studies in psychology aim to make discoveries about aspects of human behaviour that can be generalised to the population under investigation. In the vast majority of cases, it would not be possible or sensible to try to involve every member of a population in a study. The alternative is to take a representative sample from the population and assume that, as long as the sample is large enough and sufficiently diverse, the data collected are a good representation of patterns of results that would be found if the entire population were to be tested. This is a reasonable assumption to make, as long as the sample is suitably representative. The three main questions that the researcher must address are shown in Figure 2.5.

How will participants be selected?

It is extremely rare that the sample of participants in a study will be a 'random' sample, so do not misuse this term. For a truly random sample to be recruited, a selection process would have been used in which every member of the population had an equal chance to be selected *and* every person selected agreed to take part in the study. In practice, neither of these things really happens in psychological research studies, so claiming that a random sample has been used in a study is best avoided, unless you can explain how this was achieved. There are various methods of sampling from the population, but they all share one common aim: to produce a representative sample in such a way as to avoid sampling bias.

> **Key term**
>
> In a **random** selection, every possible outcome has an equal chance of occurring. This term has a very specific definition and should not be used more generally to refer to a method of selection that does not satisfy this condition.

Sampling bias

Sampling bias occurs when the way in which participants have been selected has a systematic effect on the results of the study through there being an over-representation of one or more categories of participant in the sample. If, for example, I wanted to investigate students' attitudes towards attendance at lectures, then handing out a questionnaire during a lecture would be a form of sampling bias, because I would only be collecting the views of students who attended and, presumably, had a positive attitude towards attendance, and not those who stayed in bed because they thought that lectures were pointless. If you want a representative sample of views about Christmas, don't only recruit turkeys, as they may have particular opinions on the subject!

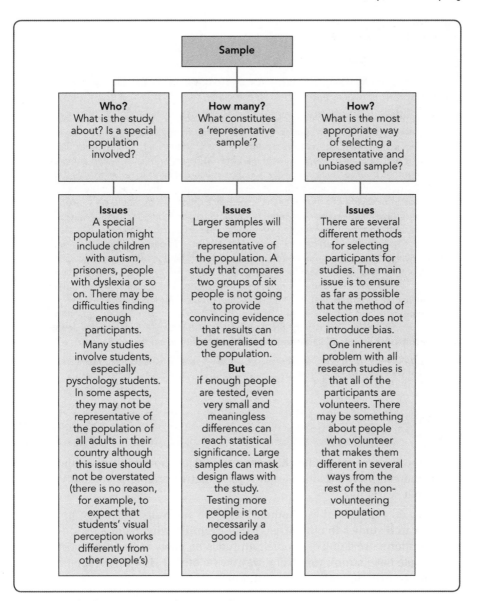

Figure 2.5 The key questions about sampling

CRITICAL FOCUS

Volunteers as participants

Please read the following and then answer the questions in the sample question box below.

> Volunteer bias in sexuality research employing college student samples has been documented in previous research. In the current study, such potential volunteer bias was further investigated, as was respondents' self-reported level of emotional discomfort during participation. College student men ($n = 310$) and women ($n = 399$) completed an anonymous questionnaire and were asked to indicate their willingness to volunteer for a similar questionnaire study, a study involving similar questions but administered in a face-to-face interview, and a study in which sexually explicit videos would be viewed. Nearly all of the men and women indicated willingness to participate in a similar questionnaire study, but more men than women were willing to participate in the other two studies. Of these two proposed studies, men were more interested in participating in the video study whereas women were more interested in participating in the interview study. Compared to nonvolunteers, volunteers for either study were generally more sexually experienced, held less traditional sexual attitudes, scored higher on measures of sexual esteem and sexual sensation seeking, and indicated greater tendencies toward interpersonal exploitation and self-monitoring of expressive behavior. A minority indicated some discomfort while completing the current questionnaire. However, discomfort was unrelated to gender or willingness to participate in future studies.

Source: Wiederman, M. (1999). Volunteer bias in sexuality research using college student participants. *Journal of Sex Research, 36*(1) 59–66.

 Sample question   *Assessment*

1 If the subsequent studies had been conducted, how might the sample of volunteers have provided an unrepresentative sample of student views about sexuality?

2 How do you think these findings might be generalisable to psychological research studies in other areas? (For example, why might a questionnaire study of people's attitudes be likely to find that most people have strong views, one way or the other? How might sampling bias contribute to this type of finding?)

Sampling methods

It is important to know about different types of sampling methods and why they would be used, but it is equally important to be aware that, when it comes to explaining how participants were selected to take part in a study, a clear explanation of how this was achieved is just as important as giving the method the correct name. In fact, a clear account without the correct label is far more informative and useful than the correct name without the explanation (e.g. 'Opportunity sampling was used' does not explain anything to the reader about how this was achieved).

The main sampling methods and their characteristics are summarised in Table 2.1.

Table 2.1 Characteristics of main sampling methods

Method	Characteristics
Simple random	Every member of the population has an equal chance of being selected. As mentioned earlier, this rarely happens in psychological research studies.
Systematic random	Selecting, for example, every fifth name from a list or knocking on every third door in a street. The starting point must be randomised or else the first name or door would always be selected and the second one never would.
Stratified random	Identifying subgroups in the population and randomly selecting from within them in proportion to the population. e.g. if the workforce of a company is 40% full-time and male, 30% full-time and female, 20% part-time and male, then the sample should reflect these proportions. Individuals would be randomly selected from each of the four groups.
Cluster	Selecting groups of participants to represent the subgroups in the population. If wanting to compare psychology students with history students, an entire class of each might be selected as participants instead of randomly selecting individuals from a list.
Quota	This is often employed in market research. It is similar to stratified sampling, in that a sample is selected that represents proportions of characteristics in the population, but the selection methods are not random.
Self-selecting	In naturalistic observational studies, the researcher cannot control who is observed. For example, if observing driver behaviour at traffic lights, the participants are self-selecting in that anyone who drove up to the traffic lights would become a participant in the study.
Opportunity or convenience	Testing the most convenient participants available, such as students attending a lecture.
Haphazard	Going to a location, such as a canteen or library, and inviting participation from anyone who happens to be there. Ideally, everyone in the location should have an equal chance of being selected.
Snowball	Asking participants to recruit further participants by word-of-mouth. This can be useful when dealing with a sensitive topic area or a vulnerable sample. For example, people engaged with using illegal drugs may be reluctant to volunteer, but may be more likely to do so once one of their friends has already taken part.

Further reading Sampling

Topic	Key reading
Explores how different sampling methods can produce different findings	Ray, J. (1983). A comparison between cluster and 'random' sampling. *Journal of Social Psychology, 121*(1), 155.

Test your knowledge

2.13 Explain, with your own examples, what is meant by 'sampling bias'

2.14 All participants in psychological research are volunteers. In what ways might this be a problem for obtaining a representative sample?

Answers to these questions can be found on the companion website at: **www.pearsoned.co.uk/psychologyexpress**

Chapter summary – pulling it all together

→ Can you tick all the points from the revision checklist at the beginning of this chapter?

→ Attempt the sample question from the beginning of this chapter using the answer guidelines below.

→ Go to the companion website at www.pearsoned.co.uk/psychologyexpress to access more revision support online, including interactive quizzes, flashcards, You be the marker exercises as well as answer guidance for the Test your knowledge and Sample questions from this chapter.

Further reading for Chapter 2	
Topic	Key reading
Common issues and problems in reporting psychological studies	Banyard, P., & Hunt, N. (2000). Reporting research: Something missing? *The Psychologist, 13*(2), 68–71.

Answer guidelines

 Sample question   *Problem-based learning*

The following is based on Hurlbert, A. C., & Ling, Y. (2007). Biological components of sex differences in color preference. *Current Biology, 17*(16), R623–R625.

Hurlbert and Ling (2007) tested 28 British females, 25 British males, 18 Chinese females and 19 Chinese males, aged 20–26, on a colour-preference task. The task involved selecting which of two colours they preferred as the colours appeared in pairs on a computer screen. Participants performed the task on two occasions, two weeks apart.

British female participants showed a preference for reddish-purple colours, and British males showed a preference for blue-green, albeit with a weaker preference than that shown by females. Chinese participants of both sexes showed a preference for reddish colours.

The preferences of female participants remained more stable across the two-week period than the preferences of the male participants.

Hurlbert and Ling 'speculate that this sex difference arose from sex-specific functional specializations in the evolutionary division of labour. The hunter-gatherer theory proposes that female brains should be specialized for gathering-related tasks' and have 'evolved to facilitate the identification of ripe, yellow fruit or edible red leaves embedded in green foliage'. They also offer an alternative explanation, which is that females 'need to discriminate subtle changes in skin color due to emotional states and social-sexual signals; again, females may have honed these adaptations for their roles as care-givers and "empathizers"'.

1 Evaluate the explanations offered by Hurlbert and Ling for their findings.
2 Develop research hypotheses from the two explanations, and devise studies to test those hypotheses. What elements must be considered in designing the studies, and how would you address them?

Approaching the question

The question asks you to consider the research findings of Hurlbert and Ling (2007) and devise studies to investigate the theories that they suggest. The key is to be very systematic and show that you understand all of the principles of design covered in this chapter.

Important points to include

- The starting point is to think about the conclusions drawn by Hurlbert and Ling. Particularly, think about what they have measured in their study and compare it with their suggested reasons for their findings. When suggesting studies to test their theories, pay attention to the definition of a good theory and the characteristics of testable hypotheses.

- Make sure that you explain as fully as you can the ways in which hypotheses can be untestable. You will need to give operational definitions for whatever it is that you wish to measure. It is important to make sure that you use the term and explain what operational definitions are.

- This type of question is inviting you to demonstrate your knowledge and understanding of all of the key concepts, so make sure that you don't miss anything out!

- Finally, give some consideration to the sample, the sample size and the sampling method (who, how many and how). Identify the most appropriate sampling method; when designing hypothetical studies like this, allow yourself the luxury of using the most ideal sampling method, but don't get carried away with using enormous numbers of participants. There is such a thing as too big a sample size, so be sensible.

- All the way through your answer, make sure that you explain and justify the decisions that you make about the study. What you would do is less important than your reasons for doing it that way (and not doing it differently).

Make your answer stand out

You can make your answer stand out by considering the broader issues raised by the research reported by Hurlbert and Ling. Consider the evolutionary explanations that they propose for their findings. Is this type of theory directly testable? Think in terms of the falsifiability of a theory that, basically, states there are evolutionary causes for some aspects of human behaviour, but these behaviours will have been modified through culture and social learning by the individual. From your other studies of psychology, there may be other 'theories' that seem to provide explanations but which are not directly testable. If you can bring any of these in to your answer as examples of theories with similar issues to those explored by Hurlbert and Ling, then this will show that you have thought more broadly about the bigger issues about the testing of theories in psychology.

Explore the accompanying website at www.pearsoned.co.uk/psychologyexpress

→ Prepare more effectively for exams and assignments using the answer guidelines for questions from this chapter.

→ Test your knowledge using multiple choice questions and flashcards.

→ Improve your essay skills by exploring the You be the marker exercises.

Notes

Notes

3

The basics of experimental design

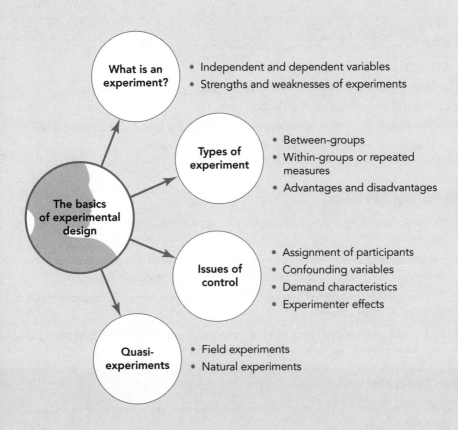

- **What is an experiment?**
  - Independent and dependent variables
  - Strengths and weaknesses of experiments

- **Types of experiment**
  - Between-groups
  - Within-groups or repeated measures
  - Advantages and disadvantages

- **The basics of experimental design**

- **Issues of control**
  - Assignment of participants
  - Confounding variables
  - Demand characteristics
  - Experimenter effects

- **Quasi-experiments**
  - Field experiments
  - Natural experiments

A printable version of this topic map is available from
www.pearsoned.co.uk/psychologyexpress

Introduction

Since the earliest days, experimental studies have been the mainstay of modern psychology. Even today, a large proportion of research studies in psychology are experiments of one type or another. Consequently, an understanding of experiments and how they are designed and carried out is crucial for any student of psychology. You need to be able not only to define key terms correctly, but also to show that you have a good understanding of all of the issues concerning experimentation in psychology. The defining characteristics of an experiment, issues in controlling an experiment and the difference between true experiments and 'quasi-experiments' are all core aspects to understanding the role that experimental studies play in psychology.

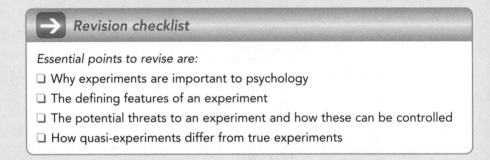

Essential points to revise are:

❏ Why experiments are important to psychology

❏ The defining features of an experiment

❏ The potential threats to an experiment and how these can be controlled

❏ How quasi-experiments differ from true experiments

Assessment advice

- You may have been asked to design an experiment, collect data and write a report.
- Report-writing allows you to put into practice some of the principles of experimental design, but greater breadth or understanding is required.
- The underlying principles and definitions of key terms may be assessed in essay-style exam questions.
- You might also be presented with examples of experiments for you to identify key characteristics or to evaluate the design of the study.

Sample question

Could you answer this question? Below is a typical essay question that could arise on this topic.

Describe, including examples, the differences between true experiments and quasi-experiments in psychology.

Guidelines on answering this question are included at the end of this chapter, whilst further guidance on tackling other exam questions can be found on the companion website at: **www.pearsoned.co.uk/psychologyexpress**

What is an experiment?

In everyday speech, people often refer to an 'experiment' as meaning anything that they are trying out to see what happens. In scientific experiments, including those conducted by psychologists, there are some key defining features that an experiment must have. These are:

- the manipulation of a 'variable'
- the measurement of the changes caused by the manipulation of the variable
- holding constant everything apart from the variable being manipulated
- random allocation of participants to experimental 'conditions'.

So, an 'experiment' is a particular type of study, and it is particularly important not to use the term to refer to just any piece of research. When learning about psychological research methods, students often use the word 'experiment' indiscriminately, perhaps because it sounds 'scientific'. Don't do this, as it reveals that you don't really understand some of the key principles of research.

Test your knowledge

3.1 What are the key characteristics of a true experiment?

An answer to this question can be found on the companion website at: **www.pearsoned.co.uk/psychologyexpress**

Independent and dependent variables

The variable that is manipulated to see what effect it has is called the 'independent variable', and the measurement that is taken is the 'dependent variable'. It is crucial to get these terms the right way round. Students often become confused and get these mixed up. Also, it is a common error to misspell the terms 'independent' and 'dependent'. Note that neither of them includes the letter 'a'!

In the most basic experiment, the independent variable is manipulated across two 'levels', each of which is also referred to as an experimental 'condition'. This is another potential source of confusion when describing and defining experimental designs. The independent variable is the thing being manipulated, and the levels of the independent variable refer to the ways in which this is changed. For example, in an experiment to investigate the effects of eating cheese on puzzle-solving, the independent variable could be 'amount of cheese eaten' and the levels of the independent variable might be '100 grams and 1000 grams'. It would not be precise to define the independent variable as 'cheese' (this is too vague) or '100 grams of cheese or 1000 grams of cheese' (these are the levels, not the independent variable). Note that the 'amount of cheese' could be set to zero as one level of the independent variable. The most important distinction to be aware of is that the experiment with 100 grams of cheese and 1000 grams of cheese has *one* independent variable with two *levels*. There are not two independent variables.

The dependent variable in this experiment would be some measure of performance on a puzzle-solving task. There are various ways of operationally defining this. For further explanation of operational definitions, see Chapter 2 of this book!

Key terms

If you get confused about which is the **independent** and which the **dependent variable** in an experiment, one way of remembering this is that the dependent variable depends on the manipulation that takes place in the experiment. This may not be a particularly powerful aide-memoire, so the simple truth is that you should just learn which is which. The more journal articles you read that describe experimental studies, the more familiar the whole enterprise will become. Eventually, this will become second nature and you will wonder why you ever got independent and dependent variables confused!

Test your knowledge

3.2 For each of the following hypotheses:

(i) name the independent variable and the dependent variable

(ii) suggest two levels for the independent variable.

(a) People are more attracted to others who have the same colour of hair as them.

(b) Listening to loud music speeds up reactions.

(c) Exposure to sunshine increases happiness.

(d) Pain tolerance can be increased by thinking positively.

(e) Pictures are more memorable than words.

Answers to these questions can be found on the companion website at: **www.pearsoned.co.uk/psychologyexpress**

CRITICAL FOCUS

Control groups

A control group is a group of participants who experience a zero level of the independent variable. It is the comparison between the control group and the experimental group that forms the basis of the basic experimental design. Careful thought needs to be given to what the control group should consist of, as it is sometimes not as straightforward as 'doing nothing'. For example, in the experiment to determine whether eating cheese improves puzzle-solving, the example included 100 grams and 1000 grams of cheese as the two levels of the independent variable. This comparison would allow us to judge whether eating *more* cheese improves puzzle-solving, but not whether eating *any* cheese makes a difference. In order to address that question, a control group is needed. The most obvious solution would be to have a condition in which participants ate nothing, but then any differences between this group and the '100 gram of cheese' group might just be due to them eating *something*, and the fact that it was cheese might be completely irrelevant. A better control group might involve participants eating 100 grams of something other than cheese to rule out the possibility that it is just the act of eating that is important.

Strengths and weaknesses of experiments

Experiments epitomise the application of scientific methods to psychology and have particular strengths.

- *Cause and effect* Experiments allow conclusions to be drawn about the causal links between independent and dependent variables.

- *Control of variables* The independent variable is manipulated and everything else, as far as possible, is held constant. This further strengthens the ability to draw conclusions about cause and effect, because alternative potential explanations can be eliminated.

- *Replicability* A key characteristic of science is that findings should be replicable. The controlled nature of an experiment means that someone else could apply the same experimental conditions and should find the same results.

Experiments also have some potential weaknesses.

- *Narrow definition of concepts* Because experiments necessitate the operational definition of concepts in order for them to be manipulated or measured, they may reduce complex behaviours and phenomena to small 'bits'.

- *Lack of ecological validity* Because experiments are artificial and take place in a laboratory, they might not provide a true reflection of the ways in which people behave in their everyday lives. Take note, however, that this criticism does not reduce all experiments to worthless exercises, so do not apply it indiscriminately to every experiment that you come across.

Key term

Ecological validity refers to the extent to which the findings of a study are applicable to everyday life. It does not necessarily follow that a laboratory experiment has less ecological validity than a more naturalistic study.

41

Types of experiment

In a basic experiment, the independent variable can be manipulated in two ways. We can either apply the two levels of the independent variable to two entirely different groups of participants or ask one group of people to experience both levels of the independent variable.

This distinction, and the terminology that goes along with it, is another very common source of confusion for students, but you should make sure that you know which is which and always use the appropriate label. Just to make matters slightly more confusing, each of the two main types of experimental design has more than one label, which can be used interchangeably. As with the difference between 'variables' and 'levels', once you understand the difference between different types of experimental design, it will become second nature. Again, the more experimental journal articles that you read, the more familiar this will become.

The terms that will be used here are 'between-groups' and 'within-groups'.

Between-groups

This is also sometimes known as 'between-subjects' or 'independent samples'. Whenever an experiment involves using different groups of participants for each level of the independent variable, it is a 'between-groups' design. So, in a between-groups design experiment, each participant experiences one level of the independent variable. In our example, each individual who takes part eats *either* 100 grams of cheese or 1000 grams of cheese. Nobody has to eat 100 grams *and* 1000 grams.

The experiment will produce two sets of scores: puzzle-solving ability scores from each of the levels of the independent variable. These two sets of scores will have come from two different sets of participants. The independent variable has been manipulated in such a way as to allow the experimenter to examine the differences in the dependent variable *between* two different groups of people, hence the term 'between-groups'.

Within-groups or repeated measures

This is also sometimes referred to as a 'related samples' design. In this type of design, every participant experiences each and every level of the independent variable. We would, therefore, need just one group of participants, with whom we would measure their puzzle-solving ability twice, once after they had eaten 100 grams of cheese and again after they had eaten 1000 grams of cheese.

In this case, the independent variable will have been manipulated *within* a single group of participants. As the same measure is being taken twice from the same group of participants, this is where the term 'repeated measures' comes from. It is not, however, necessary for the two experimental conditions to be run separately. If, for example, an experimenter wants to run a within-groups experiment to see whether people remember pictures or words better, the participants could be shown a sequence that alternates between words and pictures. In this way, both of the conditions can be run at the same time and the numbers of words and pictures recalled by each participant can be totalled up separately.

Advantages and disadvantages

There are advantages and disadvantages to between-groups and within-groups designs. They have different characteristics, which means that sometimes, a between-groups design is the best or even the only viable option, and sometimes a within-groups design is called for. If the effects of practice on a task are being investigated, then a within-groups design is the only option.

Figure 3.1 summarises the advantages and disadvantages of both types of design. The relative advantages and disadvantages of between-groups and within-groups designs are important because they relate to the control that the experimenter has over the experiment. One of the key characteristics and, indeed, the main advantages of an experiment is that it is carefully controlled so that it can be concluded that any effect observed has been caused by the manipulation of the independent variable, not by anything else.

Key terms

In a **between-groups design**, each participant is exposed to only one level of the independent variable. In a **within-groups design**, all participants experience all levels of the independent variable. It is important to remember that these terms refer exclusively to experiments. One common misunderstanding is to refer to correlational studies as 'within-groups' or 'repeated measures' designs. This is incorrect because correlational studies are not experiments.

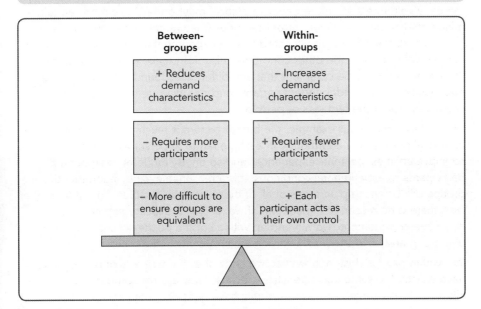

Figure 3.1 Between-groups versus within-groups designs

Test your knowledge

3.3 What are the advantages and disadvantages of between-groups and within-groups designs?

An answer to this question can be found on the companion website at:
www.pearsoned.co.uk/psychologyexpress

Issues of control

The most important principle in experimental investigations is that the only difference between experimental conditions should be the level of the independent variable. Every participant who takes part in the same experimental condition should experience the same thing. There are several key issues that are important in ensuring that the experiment is properly controlled.

Assignment of participants

In a true experiment, participants are randomly allocated to experimental conditions. The purpose of this is to eliminate any systematic differences that might result from the two groups consisting of different people with different characteristics. For example, participants who volunteer straight away to take part in an experiment might differ in some important ways from people who come along much later on. They clearly have different motivation levels, perhaps the early volunteers are more eager to please, maybe they have more enquiring minds, they might also have better memories (they remembered to volunteer!). If the first 20 volunteers are allocated to one experimental condition, and the next 20 volunteers to the other condition, this might make it very difficult for the experimenter to be confident that any differences found were due to the manipulation of the independent variable and not just due to the different characteristics of the two sets of people.

While this is an obvious example, the bigger picture is much more complex. Individual people vary enormously in a whole range of personality characteristics, cognitive abilities, personal experiences and so on. By randomly distributing participants to experimental conditions, it is a reasonable expectation that the groups will 'balance up' in terms of all of these internal variables. To put it another way, there is no reason to expect that, if we randomly allocate participants to the two 'cheese' conditions, we will end up with all of the puzzle-solving experts in one group and all of the puzzle-solving incompetents in the other.

In a within-groups design, however, we know that the two sets of participants have exactly the same characteristics, *because they are the same people*. This allows us to be confident that the results have not been influenced by any participant characteristics, as everything is automatically controlled for.

'Randomness'

In everyday speech, the word 'random' is often used to mean anything that was unexpected, previously unknown or even as an exclamation (e.g. 'This random man came up to me in the street', 'Really? Wow, random!', 'Yeah'). These nonsensical utterings do not relate in any way to the use of the word 'random' in scientific work. In terms of the allocation of participants to experimental conditions, a truly random assignment would be one in which each participant has an equal chance of being allocated to each condition, and in which it is impossible to predict to which condition each participant will be assigned.

In practice, this could produce some major problems, because it would be possible for every participant to be allocated to the *same* condition. Ideally, we would prefer our group sizes to be at least roughly equal, and we certainly need at least *some* participants in each condition! To avoid this problem, experimenters use a form of 'block randomisation'. Rather than allocate every individual participant randomly, they might be allocated in pairs, so the first volunteer will be randomly allocated, and the second will then be allocated to the other experimental condition. This is not 'true' randomness, because the assignment of participants number 2 is predictable from the assignment of participant number 1, but it is good enough in that it controls for the characteristics of the participants to avoid any systematic bias.

You may have already spotted that within-groups designs do not randomly allocate participants to conditions, because all participants experience all levels of the independent variable. Instead, participants are allocated to the *order* in which they experience each of the experimental conditions, and that allocation can be handled randomly.

 Sample question   *Assessment*

Is a within-groups experiment a true experiment? How important is this?

Confounding variables

The aim of an experiment is to manipulate the independent variable but to make sure, as far as possible, that nothing else changes. The only difference between the experimental conditions should be the level of the independent variable. A confounding variable is a variable that sneaks into the experiment unnoticed. Specifically, a confounding variable is one that affects the dependent variable and is associated in some systematic way with the independent variable. In other words, in manipulating the independent variable the experimenter has also, inadvertently, changed another variable that could also be responsible for any observed effects on the dependent variable. This makes it very difficult to draw any conclusions about the effects of manipulating the independent variable on the dependent variable. If an experiment has a confounding variable, it is said to be 'confounded'.

Key term

A **confounding variable** is something that changes systematically as the independent variable is manipulated. This term should not be used as a general term to refer to any other design flaw in an experiment.

Test your knowledge

3.4 In an investigation into the effects of seeing food-related pictures on eating behaviour, an experimenter divided participants into two groups. In the 'food' group, participants were shown 25 brightly coloured photographs of food. In the 'furniture' group, participants were shown 25 black-and-white photographs of furniture. All participants were then invited into a room and allowed to eat as many pieces of cheese as they wanted. The experimenter found that the participants who saw the photographs of food ate much more cheese than the participants who were shown the pictures of furniture.

The researcher concluded that seeing pictures of food makes people eat more. Is this conclusion valid? Is there a confounding variable, and what alternative explanation could be offered to explain the results?

Answers to this question can be found on the companion website at: **www. pearsoned.co.uk/psychologyexpress**

Demand characteristics

In psychology, experiments most often involve human participants. There is a natural tendency for people to be curious about the experiment and try to please the experimenter and help them out by behaving in the 'right way'. The information and cues that are available to participants within the experimental setting are referred to as the 'demand characteristics' of the experiment. It is important that these cues are minimised as far as possible, because the effects of the independent variable on the dependent variable cannot be isolated and identified if participants are deliberately altering their behaviour in the experiment in accordance with how they *think* they are expected to behave. One advantage of a between-groups design is that it is more difficult for participants to guess the experimental hypothesis or, in some cases, to even spot the independent variable. In within-groups designs, participants get to see more than one experimental condition and so have much more opportunity to work out what the experimenter is expecting to happen and alter their behaviour accordingly.

In some types of experiments, particularly those that make use of speeded response-time measures, it is fairly straightforward to see whether participants have deliberately tried to respond more slowly because that is what they think is expected. A deliberate attempt to slow down a response time usually produces much slower response times that reflect not just the participant's response to the stimulus, but also the time taken for them to make a decision about how slow or fast they need to be in responding.

Test your knowledge

3.5 What are demand characteristics, why are they problematic and what can be done to reduce them in an experiment?

An answer to this question can be found on the companion website at: **www.pearsoned.co.uk/psychologyexpress**

Further reading Demand characteristics

Topic	Key reading
A reprint of Orne's classic paper on demand characteristics, first published in 1962	Orne, M. (2002). On the social psychology of the psychological experiment: With particular reference to demand characteristics and their implications. *Prevention & Treatment, 5*(1), 35–45.
Overcoming demand characteristics by using false cues about the purpose of the experiment	Laney, C., Kaasa, S., Morris, E., Berkowitz, S., Bernstein, D., & Loftus, E. (2008). The red herring technique: A methodological response to the problem of demand characteristics. *Psychological Research, 72*(4), 362–375.
Factors influencing when participants comply with demand characteristics	Navarick, D. (2007). Attenuation and enhancement of compliance with experimental demand characteristics. *Psychological Record, 57*(4), 501–515.

Experimenter effects

The way in which the experimenter conducts the experiment can influence its outcomes. Experimenters make every effort to be objective and to avoid contributing to the demand characteristics of the experiment. All of the inadvertent influences that may be exerted by the experimenter are referred to as 'experimenter effects'.

Standardisation of procedures

The standardisation of procedures, as well as being a central feature of experimental work, is a key element in reducing experimenter effects. One major aspect in ensuring the standardisation of procedures is the standardisation of the instructions to participants. Most commonly, instructions are standardised by writing them down. These can either be given to participants to read or can be read out to them by the experimenter. The former removes any possibility that the experimenter's tone of voice or inadvertent emphasis on a particular word can provide additional cues to the participant.

Standardised instructions ensure that:

- the instructions are the same for all participants in the same condition
- the experimenter does not forget anything
- the experimenter does not accidentally reveal the hypothesis of the experiment.

Ensuring everything that is said and done is the same from one participant to the next reduces experimenter effects and ensures the effect of the independent variable can be isolated.

Single-blind and double-blind

In the types of experiment performed by psychologists, it is usually the case that participants are not provided with full details of the design of the experiment, the independent variables and the hypothesis before participating. In order to reduce demand characteristics, participants are not usually told which experimental condition they are in or anything about the other experimental conditions. This type of procedure is known as a 'single-blind'. The experimenter knows which condition the participant is in, but the participant does not.

In a double-blind procedure, neither the participant nor the experimenter knows to which experimental group the participant has been assigned. This is not widely used in most experimental research in psychology, partly because the measures used in psychological experiments tend not to be open to interpretation and partly because the standardisation of procedures will, in most cases, provide sufficient control of experimenter effects. In some research, however, such as medical research, the researcher may be assessing the behaviour of a patient after they have undergone either a drug treatment or treatment with a placebo drug. If the person doing the assessment has their own expectations about the effectiveness of the drug treatment, then this can influence their judgement. In such cases, neither the participant nor the person collecting the data will be told which experimental condition the participant has been assigned to. Because neither knows, this is 'double-blind'.

Test your knowledge

3.6 What are 'experimenter effects'? How can they be reduced?

An answer to this question can be found on the companion website at:
www.pearsoned.co.uk/psychologyexpress

Quasi-experiments

As already identified, a true experiment involves the manipulation of an independent variable and the random allocation of participants to experimental conditions. There are other types of studies that are very similar to experiments but do not have all of the characteristics required of a true experiment. These are referred to as 'quasi-experiments'.

Field experiments

A field experiment is one that is conducted outside the laboratory in a real-world setting. Note that 'outside the laboratory' does not just mean running a carefully controlled experiment in another room that is not a 'laboratory'; it refers to manipulating an independent variable in a situation that does not involve an artificial laboratory task in which the independent variable is isolated. Field experiments can be run in all types of settings, including a variety of workplaces, or simply out in the street.

A field experiment, then, involves the manipulation of an independent variable and the measuring of a dependent variable. The nature of the setting might not allow participants to be randomly allocated to conditions.

Field experiments have some advantages and disadvantages in comparison to laboratory-based 'true' experiments. These are summarised in Figure 3.2.

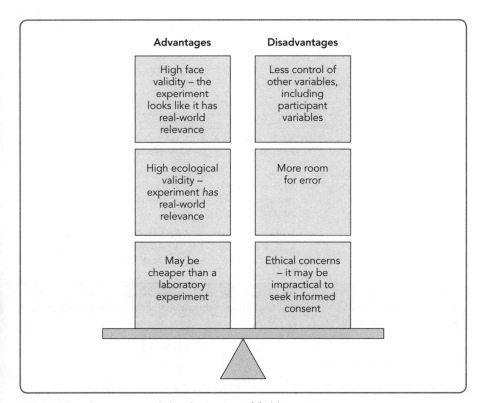

Figure 3.2 Advantages and disadvantages of field experiments

Sample question **Assessment**

Read the following abstract and answer the questions that follow.

This field study investigated the extent to which stereotypically French and German music could influence supermarket customers' selections of French and German wines. Music with strong national associations should activate related knowledge and be linked with customers buying wine from the respective country. Over a two-week period, French and German music was played on alternate days from an in-store display of French and German wines. French music led to French wines outselling German ones, whereas German music led to the opposite effect on sales of French wine. Responses to a questionnaire suggested that customers were unaware of these effects of music on their product choices. The results are discussed in terms of their theoretical implications for research on music and consumer behaviour and their ethical implications for the use of in-store music.

Source: North, A. C., Hargreaves, D. J., & McKendrick, J. (1999). The influence of in-store music on wine selections. *Journal of Applied Psychology, 84*(2), 271–276.

1 How does this differ from a laboratory experiment in terms of the recruitment of participants, their assignment to conditions?

2 What other factors might have influenced which wine customers chose to buy?

3 What advantages does this study have over a laboratory experiment?

Further reading Field experiments

Topic	Key reading
Everyday helping and prejudice	Hendren, A., & Blank, H. (2009). Prejudiced behavior toward lesbians and gay men: A field experiment on everyday helping. *Social Psychology, 40*(4), 234–238.
Influencing whether people will give directions to a stranger	Fischer-Lokou, J., Lamy, L., & Guéguen, N. (2009). Induced cognitions of love and helpfulness to lost persons. *Social Behavior & Personality: An International Journal, 37*(9), 1213–1220.
Racial discrimination in a retail setting	Schreer, G., Smith, S., & Thomas, K. (2009). 'Shopping while Black': Examining racial discrimination in a retail setting. *Journal of Applied Social Psychology, 39*(6), 1432–1444.
A classic field study of aggression in response to supermarket queue-jumping	Harris, M. (1976). Instigators and inhibitors of aggression in a field experiment. *Journal of Social Psychology, 98*(1), 27–38.

Natural experiments

A natural experiment is one that does not involve the direct manipulation of an independent variable by the experimenter. Rather, the researcher takes advantage of different 'conditions' that exist naturally in the real world. For example, Shapiro, Smith, Malone and Collaro (2010) compared the recidivism rates of juvenile offenders who had been evaluated in residential settings (e.g. a young offenders institution) with those evaluated in community settings. They did not create the two different settings and neither did they randomly allocate participants to a setting. As the two different types of evaluation were already in existence within a particular US state, Shapiro et al. were able to make the comparison between the two conditions in this natural experiment (they found, incidentally, that recidivism rates amongst first-time offenders were higher when evaluation occurred in residential settings). This example shows how natural experiments can produce useful and informative findings when to actually conduct a true experiment would be impractical and/or unethical.

The advantages and disadvantages of natural experiments are summarised in Figure 3.3.

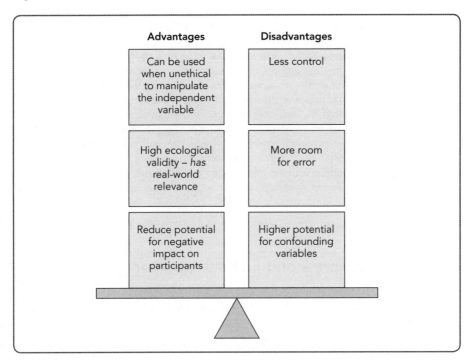

Figure 3.3 Advantages and disadvantages of natural experiments

Further reading Natural experiments

Topic	Key reading
Youth recidivism	Shapiro, C. J., Smith, B. H., Malone, P. S., & Collaro, A. L. (2010). Natural experiment in deviant peer exposure and youth recidivism. *Journal of Clinical Child & Adolescent Psychology, 39*(2), 242–251.
Weight and eating	Wardle, J., & Watters, R. (2004). Sociocultural influences on attitudes to weight and eating: Results of a natural experiment. *International Journal of Eating Disorders, 35*(4), 589–596.

Topic	Key reading
Religion, motivation and cheating	Rettinger, D. A., & Jordan, A. E. (2005). The relations among religion, motivation, and college cheating: A natural experiment. *Ethics & Behavior, 15*(2), 107–129.
Pet ownership and health	Headey, B., Nu, F., & Zheng, R. (2008). Pet dogs benefit owners' health: A 'natural experiment' in China. *Social Indicators Research, 87*(3), 481–493.

CRITICAL FOCUS

Natural experiments and group differences

A natural experiment involves making comparisons between 'experimental' conditions that have occurred 'naturally' in the real world, without the intervention of the experimenter. In psychology, there are many types of quasi-experimental study that are similar to this, but which are more laboratory based than the typical natural experiment. For example, psychology students are often interested in making comparisons between males and females in their performance on any number of different types of task or measure. Obviously, participants cannot be randomly allocated to being 'male' or 'female', and this cannot be manipulated directly by the experimenter. Therefore, rather than being a true between-groups experiment, any comparison based on the pre-existing characteristics of participants, such as gender, age, height, weight, political views, etc., is a quasi-experiment that lies somewhere between a true experiment and a natural experiment. Nothing is being manipulated and participants cannot be randomly allocated, but the study may involve a laboratory-based experimental task.

Chapter summary – pulling it all together

→ Can you tick all the points from the revision checklist at the beginning of this chapter?

→ Attempt the sample question from the beginning of this chapter using the answer guidelines below.

→ Go to the companion website at **www.pearsoned.co.uk/psychologyexpress** to access more revision support online, including interactive quizzes, flashcards, You be the marker exercises as well as answer guidance for the Test your knowledge and Sample questions from this chapter.

Further reading for Chapter 3

Topic	Key reading
Classic experiments in psychology	Slater, L. (2005). *Opening Skinner's box: Great psychological experiments of the twentieth century.* New York: W. W. Norton & Co.

Answer guidelines

 Sample question *Essay*

Describe, including examples, the differences between true experiments and quasi-experiments in psychology.

Approaching the question

The question asks you to describe the differences between experimental and quasi-experimental designs in psychology. Think very carefully about this, because the question may have hidden depths. The most obvious approach to the question would be to list the defining features of experiments and quasi-experiments, but the 'differences' being asked for might be subtler than this.

Important points to include

- Think about the question. Experiments and quasi-experiments differ in how they are defined and conducted, but they also differ in their relative strengths and weaknesses, so do not neglect this aspect, as this shows that you have a deeper understanding of the importance of asking the question. Being able to describe an experiment and a quasi-experiment is one thing, but being able to discuss why these differences matter is quite another, and is what characterises the understanding and knowledge expected at this level of study.
- Show you know 'quasi-experiment' is a term that can cover a range of different types of study and give examples to illustrate your points.
- Along the way, make sure that you show you know about variables and levels, about different types of design and about issues of control.

Make your answer stand out

You can make your answer stand out by including examples to show that you have read around the topic area and can use different types of study to illustrate the different points you are making about the relative strengths and weaknesses of experimental and quasi-experimental studies and the conclusions that can be drawn from them. The more examples that you can include, the better, especially if you are able to draw on a diverse set of recently published journal articles that show a good range of field experiment and natural experiments, as well as traditional laboratory experiments.

Explore the accompanying website at **www.pearsoned.co.uk/psychologyexpress**
→ Prepare more effectively for exams and assignments using the answer guidelines for questions from this chapter.
→ Test your knowledge using multiple choice questions and flashcards.
→ Improve your essay skills by exploring the You be the marker exercises.

Notes

4

Designing complex experiments

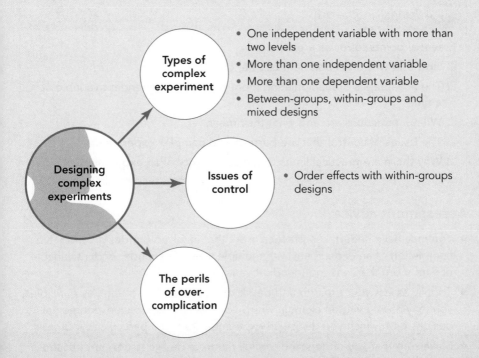

Types of complex experiment

- One independent variable with more than two levels
- More than one independent variable
- More than one dependent variable
- Between-groups, within-groups and mixed designs

Designing complex experiments

Issues of control

- Order effects with within-groups designs

The perils of over-complication

A printable version of this topic map is available from
www.pearsoned.co.uk/psychologyexpress

Introduction

It is relatively unusual for experimental studies in psychology to be of the simplest design in which one independent variable is manipulated with two levels. Much more often, experiments are more complex than this and manipulate an independent variable across three or more levels and/or employ more than one independent variable. It is important for you to understand how these types of experiment are designed and conducted and, crucially, how they allow researchers to explore complex psychological theories and constructs in ways that simple experiments do not allow. The increased complexity of these types of experiments further complicate the considerations that need to be given to the control of the experiment, and these more involved matters are ones of which you need to be able to demonstrate a sophisticated and in-depth understanding.

→ Revision checklist

Essential points to revise are:

❏ How and why an experiment can be 'complex'
❏ The advantages of manipulating more than one independent variable at a time
❏ What interactions are and what they mean
❏ The issues of control that are particular to complex experiments
❏ Why there are practical limits to the complexity of an experiment

Assessment advice

- You may have undertaken practical work that involved the design and completion of an experiment with multiple levels of an independent variable or with more than one independent variable.

- To fully assess your breadth and depth of understanding of the key principles, you may have a written exam in which you evaluate complex experimental designs or in which you devise an experiment to test a particular hypothesis.

- Make sure that you understand the full range of design issues, not just those that may have applied to your specific piece of practical work.

Sample question

Could you answer this question? Opposite is a typical problem question that could arise on this topic.

The following is based on Kenealy, P. (1997). Mood-state-dependent retrieval: The effects of induced mood on memory reconsidered. *The Quarterly Journal of Experimental Psychology A: Human Experimental Psychology, 50A*(2), 290–317.

Kenealy (1997) conducted a series of five experiments investigating the effects of mood on memory. The memory task involved learning a simple map and a set of 22 auditory instructions that related to a particular route around the map. Participants learned the map and the instructions until they could achieve at least 80 per cent accuracy. On the following day, participants were asked to recall the information. Participants were put into a happy or a sad mood before learning the information on Day 1 and again before retrieving the information on Day 2.

Some of the results of Kenealy's study are shown in Figure 4.1.

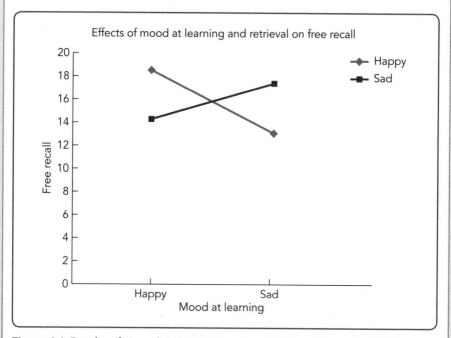

Figure 4.1 **Results of Kenealy's (1997) Experiment 3 (from Kenealy, 1997)**

1 Use your knowledge of the design of complex experiments to suggest how the experiments described above might have been conducted. Make reference to the type of design, the independent and dependent variables and to issues of control that are pertinent to this type of study.

2 Interpret the results of the experiment shown in Figure 4.1. Describe the effects of the independent variables on the dependent variable, making use of the appropriate terminology.

Guidelines on answering this question are included at the end of this chapter, whilst further guidance on tackling other exam questions can be found on the companion website at: **www.pearsoned.co.uk/psychologyexpress**

Types of complex experiment

One independent variable with more than two levels

An independent variable is not limited to having just two levels. In many cases, limiting an experiment to just two conditions can seriously affect the conclusions that can be drawn about the effects of the independent variable on the dependent variable. Take, for example, the issue of control groups, as discussed in the previous chapter. If an experimenter wanted to see if drinking a caffeinated drink improves memory for a list of words, then the experimental group might drink 250 ml of coffee before seeing the word list. If the control group does not have any drink, then any observed effects might be due to the experimental group simply having a drink (i.e. a confounding variable arises). If, however, the control group drinks 250 ml of decaffeinated coffee and the caffeinated coffee-drinkers perform better on the memory test, this would suggest that drinking a caffeinated drink does improve memory, compared with drinking a non-caffeinated drink. This would not, however, say anything about the difference between having a drink and not having a drink. The more complete experimental design would involve all three levels of the independent variable: caffeinated drink, non-caffeinated drink, no drink. If you think carefully about this, though, there is another potential confounding variable: perhaps any effects are due to the *taste* of the drink. A better design would incorporate further levels in which the amount of caffeine in the drink is increased without altering the taste. (Why wouldn't just asking participants to drink more coffee be a good idea?)

Linear and non-linear effects

The use of multiple levels of an independent variable allows the experimenter to obtain a fuller picture of exactly how the independent variable affects the dependent variable. Figure 4.2 illustrates how the judicious selection of levels of the independent variable impacts on the conclusions that can be drawn.

The careful selection of the appropriate levels of the independent variable can, therefore, be crucial in developing a theoretical account of the effect that the independent variable has on the dependent variable. Note, particularly, the different findings and conclusions from Figure 4.2(a) compared to 4.2(f). This shows, particularly, why using just two levels of an independent variable can be problematic when that variable varies on a continuum (the amount of caffeine is a continuous measure). The decisions taken about how to divide a continuous variable into levels and how to define those levels can change the results and

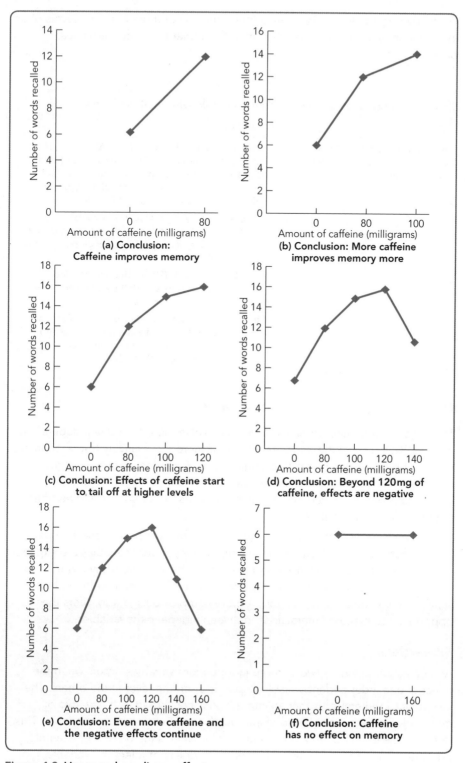

Figure 4.2 Linear and non-linear effects

conclusions quite drastically. Only through the use of more than two levels of an independent variable can it be determined whether the effects are linear or non-linear.

Further reading Single independent variable with multiple levels

Topic	Key reading
A variety of studies that manipulate one independent variable across three or more levels	Kano, M., Gyoba, J., Kamachi, M., Mochizuki, H., Hongo, M., & Yanai, K. (2003). Low doses of alcohol have a selective effect on the recognition of happy facial expressions. *Human Psychopharmacology: Clinical & Experimental, 18*(2), 131–139.
	Field, A., & Schorah, H. (2007). The verbal information pathway to fear and heart rate changes in children. *Journal of Child Psychology & Psychiatry, 48*(11), 1088–1093.
	Roth, E., & Smith, K. (2008). The Mozart effect: Evidence for the arousal hypothesis. *Perceptual & Motor Skills, 107*(2), 396–402.
	Strayer, D., Drews, F., & Johnston, W. (2003). Cell phone-induced failures of visual attention during simulated driving. *Journal of Experimental Psychology: Applied, 9*(1), 23–32.

More than one independent variable

The majority of psychological experiments involve more than one independent variable. This reflects the understanding that there are relatively few phenomena that can be best explained with a single factor. The effect of one variable might not be as simple as we would like and its effects must be explored in conjunction with other variables in order to gain a better understanding of its operation in a slightly more realistic way.

There are some distinct advantages to experiments that have more than one independent variable. Because the effects of independent variables are explored under different conditions, the experiment's results are potentially more generalisable than those from an experiment in which a single independent variable is manipulated in isolation. A more complex design also offers the opportunity to explore 'interactions' between independent variables.

Interactions

An interaction between two or more independent variables occurs when the effect of one independent variable depends upon the level of the others. The key point to remember is that an interaction is concerned with how two or more independent variables *combine* to influence the dependent variable. This does not mean that one independent variable *affects* the other. For example, presenting the name of an animal in red print does not affect the variable 'type

Combining variables

A vital feature of an experiment with more than one independent variable is that the variables are combined in experimental conditions. Take a simple example: if one independent variable is the type of word presented (animals or vegetables) and the second is the colour of the ink in which they are printed (red or blue), this gives four different combinations of word-type and colour (red animal, blue animal, red vegetable, blue vegetable). In other words, each participant in the experiment will experience (at least) one level of *both* independent variables. It is the combination of variables that is crucial and what sets this type of design apart from running two separate experiments: one comparing animal words with vegetable words and a second comparing red words with blue ones.

Note that each participant experiencing one level of each (or all) of the independent variables does not make this a within-groups design, because it does not necessarily follow that each participant experiences every *level* of each independent variable. There will be more about this later.

of word', but the combination of colour and type of word may influence the dependent variable (number of words recalled).

In a well-known experiment, Godden and Baddeley (1975) investigated the effects of learning and recalling words either on land or underwater. Divers learned a word list either on land or underwater. Half of the participants then recalled the words in the same location, while the other half recalled them in the other environment. The results are illustrated in Figure 4.3.

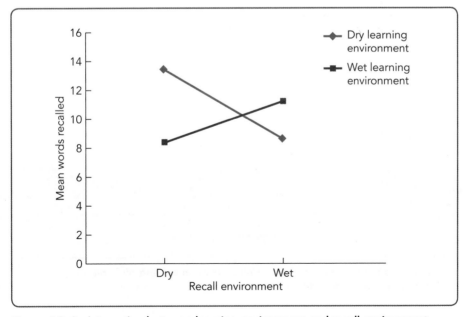

Figure 4.3 An interaction between learning environment and recall environment (from Godden & Baddeley, 1975)

This is an interaction because the effect of the location of recall is different for the two locations of learning. For the participants who learned the words on dry land, recalling on dry land was better than recalling underwater. However, for those who learned the words underwater, underwater recall was better than dry land recall. Overall, note that there is no big difference between the effectiveness of learning on dry land or learning underwater, and there is no difference between the effectiveness of recalling on dry land or recalling underwater. This is an important point, because it shows how an interaction between two independent variables can occur even when neither of them has an overall individual effect on the results. The effect that an individual independent variable has on the dependent variable is called a 'main effect'. Interactions can occur without there being a main effect of any independent variable.

In comparison, consider the results shown in Figure 4.4. These are the findings from a follow-up study by Godden and Baddeley (1980). They repeated the procedure from their earlier study but, this time, a recognition measure was used instead of a free-recall measure.

This time there was no interaction between the variables. There was a main effect of the type of learning environment (learning on dry land produced higher recognition than learning underwater), but this was the same for both levels of the other independent variable. Once participants had learned the words, it didn't make any difference where they performed the recognition task.

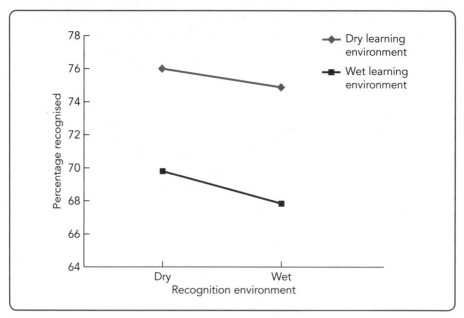

Figure 4.4 No interaction between learning environment and recognition environment (Godden & Baddeley, 1980)

When there is an interaction, the main effects of independent variables become less important than if there was no interaction. As a simple example, compare these two sets of findings:

A. Using a mobile phone while driving increases driving errors.

B. Using a mobile phone while driving increases driving errors, but only for inexperienced drivers.

Both A and B report a main effect of an independent variable, but B also incorporates an interaction. In the case of B, the fact that mobile phone use increases driving errors is less informative once we know that its effects are different at different levels of another independent variable (driving experience).

Any determination of whether there is an interaction between independent variables is a matter of statistical calculation; you cannot tell by just looking (although if lines are parallel, there is no interaction). While the calculation of statistical significance is beyond the scope of this book, the important point is that you understand the concept of interaction and how to explain it.

Key term

In experimental design, an **interaction** specifically refers to how two or more independent variables combine to influence the dependent variable. Be careful to avoid referring to this as one independent variable affecting the other. This term should also not be used more generally to refer to, for example, the differences between two experimental conditions in a simple experiment.

Further reading Experiments with multiple independent variables

Topic	Key reading
Some examples of experiments that manipulate more than one independent variable and report interactions between variables (including the Godden and Baddeley papers referred to in the text)	DeWall, C., Bushman, B., Giancola, P., & Webster, G. (2010). The big, the bad, and the boozed-up: Weight moderates the effect of alcohol on aggression. *Journal of Experimental Social Psychology, 46*(4), 619–623.
	Godden, D. R., & Baddeley, A. D. (1975). Context-dependent memory in two natural environments: On land and underwater. *British Journal of Psychology, 66*(3), 325–331.
	Godden, D. R, & Baddeley, A. D. (1980). When does context influence recognition memory? *British Journal of Psychology, 71*(1), 99–104.
	Meier, B., Robinson, M., & Caven, A. (2008). Why a Big Mac is a good Mac: Associations between affect and size. *Basic & Applied Social Psychology, 30*(1), 46–55.
	Waszak, F. (2010). Across-task long-term priming: Interaction of task readiness and automatic retrieval. *Quarterly Journal of Experimental Psychology, 63*(7), 1414–1429.

More than one dependent variable

A complex experiment can be used to investigate the effects of independent variables on more than one dependent variable at a time. This can be very efficient and time-saving, as the alternative would be to run two entirely different experiments. One of the most commonly occurring forms of this involves experiments that use response-time measures. For example, if a computer-based experiment involves looking at a series of faces and pressing a key according to whether the face is that of an actor or a politician, then the independent variable would be 'type of person'. Two dependent variables can be easily measured: the response time and the number of errors. It would be foolish to run the same experiment twice, once to measure response time and again to measure error rate. An advantage of measuring more than one dependent variable in an experiment is that the relationship between the two measures can be examined (are faster responses associated with higher error rates?).

Between-groups, within-groups and mixed designs

When more than one independent variable is manipulated in an experiment, there is the same decision to be made as with a simple experiment with one independent variable: should the variable be manipulated between-groups or within-groups? The same advantages and disadvantages of between-groups and within-groups designs apply as discussed in the previous chapter, but some of the potential difficulties can become exacerbated as more independent variables are manipulated. For instance, in a simple experiment with two conditions, a between-groups design requires twice as many participants as a within-groups design. In an experiment with two independent variables, each with two levels, if both independent variables are manipulated between-groups, *four times* as many participants would be needed compared with an experiment in which both independent variables are manipulated as within-groups. It might be tempting, therefore, to opt for a within-groups design, but the greater exposure to different experimental conditions can increase the problems associated with demand characteristics. A participant who experiences four different combinations of independent variables has a greater opportunity to guess the experimental hypotheses than a participant who takes part in just one of the four possible combinations.

When manipulating more than one independent variable, the variables do not have to be manipulated in the same way. One could be between-groups and the others within-groups. A combination of between-groups and within-groups manipulation in the same experiment is known as a 'mixed design'.

Terminology of design

In addition to the 'mixed design', the experiment with more than one independent variable generates a new set of terminology, which is often used in journal articles and other publications when reporting experiments. Psychologists (including research methods lecturers) discussing experimental studies will use these terms in conversation and it is important to understand what they mean.

As already noted, there are three main types of design: between-groups, within-groups and mixed designs. Between-groups designs are also sometimes referred to as 'factorial designs'.

If there are two independent variables, each has two levels and both are manipulated between-groups. This is referred to as a '2 × 2 between-groups design'. The '2 × 2' is pronounced 'two by two', and each of the twos refers to the number of levels of one of the independent variables. Similarly, there are '2 × 2 within-groups designs' and '2 × 2 mixed designs'. With a mixed design, additional information is needed to specify which of the independent variables is manipulated between-groups and which within-groups.

Key term

Students occasionally get confused about the **2 × 2 design** and think that the first '2' refers to the levels of the independent variable and the second '2' refers in some way to the dependent variable. This results in them trying to apply this type of terminology inappropriately to an experiment that has only one independent variable.

Test your knowledge

4.2 For each of the following designs, specify (i) the number of independent variables, (ii) the number of levels of each of the independent variables and (iii) how many participants would be needed if there were 20 in each of the experimental conditions.

(a) A 2 × 2 between-groups design.
(b) A 3 × 2 within-groups design.
(c) A 2 × 2 × 2 between-groups design.
(d) A 2 × 2 mixed design.
(e) A 5 × 2 × 2 × 2 between-groups design.

Finally, why does the following make no sense?
(f) A 1 × 2 between-groups design.

Answers to these questions can be found on the companion website at: **www.pearsoned.co.uk/psychologyexpress**

Issues of control

Issues of control with complex experiments are very similar to those raised with simpler designs, although, as already noted, there may be a need to pay even more careful attention to demand characteristics. Also, as the complexity of an experiment increases and more groups of participants are required to fill the different combinations of independent variables (or multiple levels of one independent variable), the challenges of ensuring the equivalence of participants in different groups can be more problematic.

The use of within-groups designs in complex experiments can also introduce some important issues about the order in which participants are exposed to the various combinations of the levels of the independent variables.

Order effects with within-groups designs

If there are multiple levels of an independent variable, multiple combinations of two or more independent variables or a combination of the two, then problems can arise if careful consideration is not given to the effects that exposure to multiple conditions might have on participants' performance. In addition to demand characteristics, there can be issues with practice effects, in which the performance of participants on a task improves as they become more familiar with it. This has the potential to be a confounding variable. If every participant experiences the same levels of the independent variable in the same order, then higher scores might be found in the later conditions and it would be impossible to determine whether this had been caused by the manipulation of the independent variable or by practice effects. There are several ways in which order effects can be reduced.

Counterbalancing

The simplest form of control is to counterbalance the order in which participants experience the different levels of the independent variable. If there are two levels of an independent variable, half of the participants would be exposed to level A first and the other half would experience level B first. This would balance up the practice effects across the two levels of the independent variable and mean that any effects found could be attributed to the manipulation of the independent variable. However, with more complex designs it is not quite so straightforward. With just two levels, there are just two possible orders. With three levels there are six possible orders, with four levels there are 24, with five there are a whopping 120 different possible orders. Many experiments will not have anything like as many as 120 participants, so attempting to counterbalance order effects by dividing participants into 120 subgroups becomes impossible. Besides anything else, it does not really make much sense for any of the potential orders to have just one participant in it.

Randomisation of condition order: the Latin square

With complex experimental designs, the counterbalancing of condition order becomes much less straightforward. There is still a need to make sure that any potential carry-over effects from one condition to the next are avoided as far as possible. One way of controlling for these factors is to use a 'Latin square'. A Latin square is a set of possible sequences of experimental conditions that has the following parameters:

- As the name implies, it's square! This means that if we have four different conditions, then there will be 4 different possible orders, rather than all of the 24 possible combinations. (In case you are wondering, it's called a 'Latin' square simply because it uses letters from the Latin alphabet to represent the elements, rather than using numbers or Greek letters.)
- Each of the four conditions will appear just once in each of the four positions in the sequence.
- Where there is an even number of conditions, each will follow each of the others exactly once. This produces a 'balanced' Latin square, but this third condition cannot be met when there is an odd number of conditions.

Here is an example of a balanced Latin square for an experiment with four conditions (labelled as A, B, C and D). Each row (i.e. reading across from left to right) represents one order in which the conditions would be experienced by a participant. Note how this Latin square satisfies the conditions above.

```
A  B  C  D
B  D  A  C
C  A  D  B
D  C  B  A
```

Participants would be allocated to one of these four orders, so, for counterbalancing to work in this way, the number of participants would need to be a multiple of four. Note that the letters A, B, C, D could correspond to four levels of one independent variable or to the four combinations of two independent variables in a 2 × 2 within-groups design. The same principles apply of ensuring that each combination of variables appears once in each position and it follows each other combination exactly once.

An example of a study that used a Latin square to counterbalance the order of experimental conditions is reported by Huber, Taffinder, Russell and Darzi (2003). They investigated the performance of surgeons undertaking keyhole surgery under a range of viewing conditions. In the study, surgeons had to perform tasks involving pulling and cutting threads under four different conditions.

A. Using equipment that allowed a 3D image to be perceived.

B. Using the same 3D equipment, but on its 2D setting.

C. Using less advanced equipment that provided a 2D image.

D. In an 'open box' view that allowed the surgeon a direct view without needing to use any viewing equipment.

All participants undertook all four of the conditions and the order in which they did so was determined by a Latin square, such as the one shown above. If the four conditions had been undertaken in the same order by all participants (e.g. A B C D), then, inevitably, performance would have increased through practice. By the time participants got to condition D, they would have become more adept at pulling and cutting the threads and so performance would have increased. This would have artificially inflated the scores in condition D and made condition A look like it was the worst one. The use of a Latin square helps to control for practice effects, as it means that, across the sample of participants, each of the four conditions occurred in each of the four positions in the sequence. This means that, when the performance within each condition is examined, the practice effects will balance out and so any remaining differences will reflect the differences in the ease of use of each of the four methods of performing surgery.

It is important to appreciate that the allocation of participants to different orders in this way does not constitute an independent variable. It might be tempting to think that the experiment would then become a between-groups design because of these subgroupings of participants, but the fact remains that all participants experience all levels of the independent variable, so the experiment is a within-groups design. At the end of the experiment, all of the data collected within each experimental condition will be combined and the order effects should all balance out, so any remaining effects that are found can be attributed to the manipulation of the independent variable(s).

> ## Test your knowledge
>
> **4.3** What is counterbalancing, what is it intended to achieve and how can it be applied to an experiment with a complex design?
>
> **4.4** Explain why dividing participants into subgroups using a Latin square procedure is not the same as the experiment having a between-groups design.
>
> Answers to these questions can be found on the companion website at:
> **www.pearsoned.co.uk/psychologyexpress**

Asymmetrical order effects

The counterbalancing of the order of the experimental conditions in a within-groups design assumes that the carry-over effects from one condition to another will be symmetrical. In some experiments, this might not be the case. For example, if an experiment is testing the hypothesis that performance of a task will be worse under one experimental condition than another, then the order in which the conditions are experienced by participants may affect the results, even if the order is counterbalanced. If participants experience the 'easier' condition first, then they should, as predicted, perform well on the task. These 'easy' conditions provide participants with an opportunity to get a lot of practice on the task, so when they subsequently undertake the same task under the more difficult conditions, they will be helped along by the valuable practice that they already had. If, on the other hand, participants undertake the more difficult condition first, then their opportunity to gain practice on the task will be interfered with and so when they later undertake the task under the easier conditions, their performance will increase, but they will not benefit from practice to the same extent as the participants who undertook the conditions in the opposite order.

This issue also generalises to more complex experiments with more conditions and these are controlled by the use of a Latin square. In the Huber et al. (2003) study of surgeons, described earlier, their application of a Latin square to counterbalance practice effects relies on the assumption that practice effects are symmetrical. It might be, for example, that undertaking condition A provides excellent practice for undertaking condition B, but that condition B might be harder and so might not provide the same degree of practice that can be carried over to Condition A. As a result, careful consideration needs to be given to carry-over effects from one condition to another before employing a Latin square to counterbalance order.

Test your knowledge

4.5 What are asymmetrical order effects and what challenges do they provide to the control of an experiment?

An answer to this question can be found on the companion website at:
www.pearsoned.co.uk/psychologyexpress

Randomisation of items

A within-groups design does not necessarily mean that participants take part in one condition, then take part in another, followed by a third. In many experiments, the different levels of the independent variable can be presented at the same time as a randomised sequence. Take, for example, the experiment mentioned earlier in which participants are asked to classify faces as either actors or politicians. It wouldn't actually make a lot of sense to present all of the actors' faces first followed by all of the politicians' faces. They have to be mixed together into a single set. In this way, both levels of the independent variable are employed simultaneously. The same idea can be extended to experiments with two or more independent variables where the two independent variables refer to characteristics of individual stimuli to be presented to participants. Whenever an experiment consists of responses to sets of individual stimuli, they can be presented in a random order. This overcomes problems with practice effects. Although participants may become faster (due to practice) or slower (due to momentary loss of concentration) in their responses as the experiment progresses, these fluctuations will apply equally across all of the experimental conditions and so will not produce any systematic bias.

The perils of overcomplication

In theory, there are no limits to the number of independent variables in an experiment or to the number of levels that each one might have. In practice, though, it is not a good idea to overcomplicate experimental designs because it can make it extremely difficult to interpret the results. If you look in published journal articles that report psychological experiments, the majority will tend to have two or three independent variables and there will rarely be anything more complicated than a 3 × 2 design. There is more scope for multiple levels when the experiment has just one independent variable, because the difficulties of analysis and interpretation arise when there are interactions between multiple variables.

An experiment with a 4 × 3 × 2 × 2 between-groups design could produce a four-way interaction between all of the variables. This would mean that the interaction between two variables is different at each level of the third and this combined effect of three independent variables is different at each level of the fourth. It would be extremely difficult, if not impossible, to interpret what all of this means in terms of how the independent variables combine to affect the dependent variable.

When planning an experiment with a complex design, especially if more than one independent variable is involved, it is essential to consider how the results can be interpreted before proceeding. It is also worth remembering that increasing the numbers of independent variables and levels can result in an enormous sample of participants being required. In the example given above, a 4 × 3 × 2 × 2 between-groups design would produce 48 different conditions. Even with a relatively modest sample size of 15 participants per group, a total of 720 participants would be needed.

Chapter summary – pulling it all together

➔ Can you tick all the points from the revision checklist at the beginning of this chapter?

➔ Attempt the sample question from the beginning of this chapter using the answer guidelines below.

➔ Go to the companion website at www.pearsoned.co.uk/psychologyexpress to access more revision support online, including interactive quizzes, flashcards, You be the marker exercises as well as answer guidance for the Test your knowledge and Sample questions from this chapter.

Further reading for Chapter 4

Topic	Key reading
Classic experiments in psychology	Mook, D. (2004). *Classic experiments in psychology.* Westport, CT: Greenwood Press.

Answer guidelines

 Sample question   *Problem-based learning*

The following is based on Kenealy, P. (1997). Mood-state-dependent retrieval. The effects of induced mood on memory reconsidered. *The Quarterly Journal of Experimental Psychology, 50*(2), 290–317.

Kenealy (1997) conducted a series of five experiments investigating the effects of mood on memory. The memory task involved learning a simple map and a set of 22 auditory instructions that related to a particular route around the map. Participants learned the map and the instructions until they could achieve at least 80 per cent accuracy. On the following day, participants were asked to recall the information. Participants were put into a happy or a sad mood before learning the information on Day 1 and again before retrieving the information on Day 2.

Some of the results of Kenealy's study are shown in Figure 4.1.

1 Use your knowledge of the design of complex experiments to suggest how the experiments described above might have been conducted. Make reference to the type of design, the independent and dependent variables and to issues of control that are pertinent to this type of study.

▶

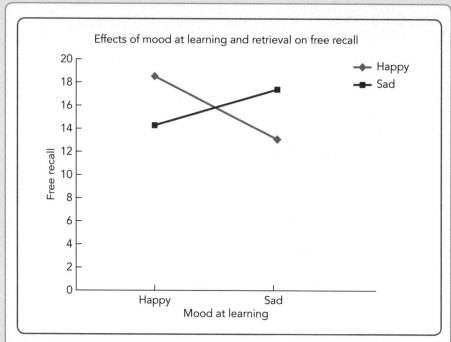

Figure 4.1 Results of Kenealy's (1997) Experiment 3 (from Kenealy, 1997)

2 Interpret the results of the experiment shown in Figure 4.1. Describe the effects of the independent variables on the dependent variable, making use of the appropriate terminology.

Approaching the question

The question involves considering a piece of published research and suggesting the most effective way of conducting the experiment. In other words, you should be able to work out how Kenealy performed these experiments. This is a slightly unusual way of presenting this type of question, but, if you think about it, it is really no different from being asked to design an experiment from scratch. The same considerations apply. The second part of the question asks you to examine the data and describe the results using the appropriate terminology. This question is tapping into your understanding of the concepts of complex experiments without necessarily asking you to become involved in the considerations of statistical analysis.

Important points to include

- Without actually giving away the 'answer', the key to considering this problem question is to put yourself in the position of the experimenter. Forget for the moment that you are being asked to comment on an existing study and ask yourself how you would design an experiment to explore the issues that Kenealy was investigating. What considerations do you need to think about?

- Start at the beginning with the independent variables, how they are defined and their levels. Show that you understand the complex nature of the experiment by considering the possible designs (between-groups, within-groups or a mixed design). How could each one be applied to this experiment? What would be the advantages and disadvantages of each and what would the procedure involve, depending on your choice?

- Think about the issues of control that are relevant to each type of design and how participants would be allocated to experimental conditions to avoid systematic bias. You should be getting the idea now that there is actually quite a lot to say here because, although it might be fairly obvious to you what the best type of design would be, you need to explain and justify your decisions and show that you know why alternative designs might not be as successful.

- In the second part of the question, focus specifically on what experiments with two independent variables can tell you that single-factor experiments cannot. Make sure that you are precise in your explanation and interpretation of the findings as shown in the graph and that you do not fall into the common traps of expressing the relevant matters in vague terms that are not totally accurate.

Make your answer stand out

You can make your answer stand out by exploring all of the possible alternative experimental designs systematically and carefully. Give full consideration to all of the appropriate issues of control. You might give examples of other complex experiments that you know about, either from your research methods work or from your studies in other areas of psychology, and discuss how they were able to use a particular type of design to test a particular hypothesis in ways that are similar to or different from the study being addressed in the question. This would demonstrate an impressive depth and breadth of knowledge and understanding.

Explore the accompanying website at www.pearsoned.co.uk/psychologyexpress
- → Prepare more effectively for exams and assignments using the answer guidelines for questions from this chapter.
- → Test your knowledge using multiple choice questions and flashcards.
- → Improve your essay skills by exploring the You be the marker exercises.

Notes

5

Case studies, single-case and small-*N* designs

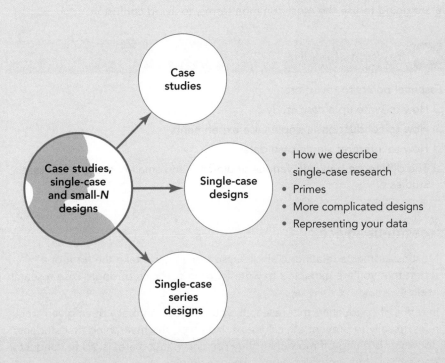

Case studies

Case studies, single-case and small-*N* designs

Single-case designs
- How we describe single-case research
- Primes
- More complicated designs
- Representing your data

Single-case series designs

A printable version of this topic map is available from
www.pearsoned.co.uk/psychologyexpress

Introduction

There are many ways to study human behaviour and not all of them involve hundreds of participants and statistical analyses. In this chapter we explain the things you need to know about case studies, single-case designs and single-case series designs. There are many names for these designs involving one or a few participants so, for your information, you will probably encounter the following terms in your reading:

- *N*-equals-one designs
- small-*N* designs
- single-subject designs
- own-control designs
- single-case designs.

We are going to use the most common terms, to avoid confusion.

> **→ Revision checklist**
>
> *Essential points to revise are:*
> ❏ How to write up a case study
> ❏ How to conduct basic single-case experiments
> ❏ How to interpret single-case data
> ❏ The difference between various single-case and small-*N* designs and case studies

Assessment advice

- Most assessments relating to single-case research will take the form of a report that you are expected to write following a piece of single-case research itself.

- In terms of conducting that research, you will have normally been given strict rules, usually to prevent ethical issues. However, the main thing that students do wrong is biting off more than they can chew. If you are asked to conduct a single-case study and report on it, keep it simple.

- Choose a common, harmless behaviour (leaving the toilet seat up or making the bed in the morning) and find a way to introduce an equally harmless 'intervention' (it could be a sticky note on the bathroom wall or the headboard of the bed). Keep your measure of the behaviour as simple and well defined as possible. Leaving the toilet seat up *seems* simple enough, but is it? Over what period of time? Do you count remembering and going back to put it down? How long between forgetting and remembering counts as failure? What happens if you find yourself using other toilets because you are out of the house more often than you expected? Would the same expectations apply? Similarly, what counts as making the bed? Pulling the duvet loosely over the bed is not the same as making sure it is lined up with equal overhang at all sides of the bed, ruffling up the pillows and so on. In these cases, the behaviour is simple, but the measurement of that behaviour is far from basic.

- When you write up, use a template that you have been given or base your format on published research. Try not to invent your own way to present things unless the research truly demands it.

Sample question

Could you answer this question? Below is a typical essay question that could arise on this topic.

 Sample question   *Essay*

Using examples, show how single-case research can be experimental.

Guidelines on answering this question are included at the end of this chapter, whilst further guidance on tackling other exam questions can be found on the companion website at: **www.pearsoned.co.uk/psychologyexpress**

Case studies

Case studies are write-ups of a history of the behaviour of a particular person, commonly used by clinical psychologists and other health professionals. They are principally nothing more than observation, although a case study approach could be used to describe an intervention being used in a scenario involving a single client or patient. Case studies are not the same thing as case notes, although case notes are used to form a case study. Case notes are the notes on a client or patient that a health professional writes. They are confidential, although legally the client can ask to see them. They can be as brief or as lengthy as suits the style of the health professional. They are only intended as an aide memoir for the psychologist or physician. Case studies are a much more public description of a case. They are intended specifically for other health professionals to learn from, to help them carry out their future work. Case notes would never be published, whereas case studies are written for that express purpose.

? *Sample question* **Assessment**

Samuel has been experiencing problems with a mouse in his kitchen, which he believes is attracted by the smells of his plug-in household air freshener. How would you devise either a case study or single-case design to explore what is happening in the mouse's behaviour?

Whilst case studies are varied in how they could, theoretically, be written up, there are a few rules to follow that seem sensible and appear to permeate the published work. In many ways, case study write-up rules are common sense, so nothing here will surprise you.

- Start with some background. Tell us about the history of the person in the case study. What age, sex, social class are they? When did they come to you? What triggered them to come to you? What are their family circumstances? What do they do for a living?

- Explain the nature of the 'problem'. This might be a particular set of clinical symptoms or it might be, in the case of coaching, a particular task a person was experiencing in their work, for example.

- Explain the intervention that was employed in this particular case. It can range from a simple half-hour discussion of the problem right through to five years of weekly therapy.

- Give the results of the intervention, as you see it. Explain the differences in the behaviour of the individual between first seeing them and after the intervention has been applied.

- Maintain anonymity and confidentiality throughout. Just giving someone a pseudonym alone does not preserve their identity, especially where you have a very specific case study and the details provided would allow someone who knew the person to identify them in the case study. The more detail you give, the easier it is to work out who the person might be. This is important. In the UK, there are 60 million people or so. By stating that someone is female, you narrow it to 30 million. That's not a problem right now. However, you then say they are 48 years old. If someone has the population statistics, that means we have narrowed it down to a much, much smaller number. For argument's sake, let's say 325,000. You then say she is the managing director of a national company selling cheeses. It suddenly jumps to *two* people. Just two. Then you say she has a husband and two children and a dog. Any reasonably skilled private detective could find out who that was. Therefore, only give detail that is *needed* to understand the case. You are not writing a novel; character development is only *partly* required.

- Try to maintain as much objectivity as possible. State the facts and make it clear when you stray into your *interpretation* of the facts. Strive to be aware of the difference, because not everyone can.

- Refer to relevant theory and published material, so that your case study is grounded and helps to add to a growing body of evidence on a subject.

Dreams and eating disorders

Roger Knudson's case study of a woman with anorexia and her dreams is an interesting window on case study method in a therapeutic context and in the use of dreams to unveil concerns. Stephanie was battling with anorexia nervosa, but had given up with her therapist because the therapist was very insistent that Stephanie should be seeking hospital help. At the time of the dream that Stephanie had, she was so underweight that her life was actually at risk (which could explain the therapist's concern).

Stephanie dreamt that her room had a wall missing and her father was dressed very oddly to go to work. There was a monster in her swimming pool, which she could see from the hole in her bedroom wall. The monster jumped up from the pool to her room. She was forced to remain silent, trying not to be seen by the monster, and knowing her life was in danger. She realises that she has to deal with the monster and to look at it. She turns towards it and wakes up.

She went back to the therapist at this point, but the therapist offered the obvious interpretation (which of course could well be true) and again was keen to have Stephanie go to hospital. She rejected this once more.

Knudson discusses the various stances that have been taken on dreams and their interpretation, pointing out that dreams are not necessarily representations of reality and are not necessarily in a logical order. Therefore, his view is that the dream must be accepted for what it is; he argues that this is an epiphany in Stephanie's life, but that telling her what it means was not a suitable approach. What Knudson focuses on, which the original therapist didn't, is Stephanie's *reaction* to the dream when she awoke, not the dream itself. She was already very conscious of the fact that her life was in danger. The dream did not *reveal* that. However, the fact that she had such vivid sensations in the dream and on waking made her realise that she was still alive, still capable of feeling and therefore *not beyond help*. To cut a longer story short, she began to gain weight and her condition improved.

We must always, it is argued, focus on what something means to our clients, not what it means to us. This might seem obvious, but many therapists and researchers forget this from time to time.

Source: Knudson, R. M. (2006). Anorexia dreaming: A case study. *Dreaming*, 16, 43–52.

Single-case designs

There is literally an infinite number of single-case designs. It is possible to keep on adding bits to a design, indefinitely. However, the more complicated something becomes, the more unwieldy and hard to interpret it gets. For that reason, most single-case designs are constrained and fairly simple as a result. Here we will focus on the basics of what you need to know.

Single-case designs are based on a simple premise. If something is real, you ought to be able to see it or at least to detect it. If it is real and meaningful, it should not need you to look hard for it. Sidman (1960) points out, therefore, that effects which are real and meaningful show up in very small numbers of participants, often as low as one. If you think of the most solid findings in psychology, they are very easy to demonstrate and you do not need hundreds or even thousands of participants. For example, people tend to remember the first and last items in a list you give to them. They forget the ones in the middle. Try it. Take a list of 15 words and read them to one person, telling them to try to remember the words. Then, get them to write down which they remember. They will almost certainly have the first two or three and the last two or three. You will struggle to find a person who remembers most items from the middle and none from the start and the end. Now, if you can show this clearly with a single participant, why waste time and resources on hundreds?

Single-case designs are intended for such situations, where you feel that an effect is robust, strong and large. However, most of the time they are used where large numbers of participants simply don't exist. If you are looking to see what happens if you apply a particular treatment to a very rare disease, for instance, you can work only with the people who have that disease. There might only be three in the country. So the single-case design could be used to plot what happens to the course of the disease when you apply the treatment. Complicated statistics simply don't play a part here. You should be aware, however, that single-case research can be just as scientific, controlled and 'experimental' as larger studies. If you try to keep confounding variables to a minimum and you systematically apply your intervention, then, arguably, the method is still scientific.

You can measure as many dependent variables as you like in single-case research. For example, a particular intervention might conceivably work in a number of ways, to improve self-esteem or a physical condition measured in a number of ways and so on. There is no limit to the number of dependent variables you can have in a single-case study other than the sheer workload of your participant having to fill in lots of questionnaires and the like.

How we describe single-case research

We use a particular nomenclature to describe the phases of single-case research. The first measurements taken need to be to establish a baseline response. This is what your participant is usually like. We call this A. At this stage, all you do is take measurements.

Key term

The **baseline** is the initial measurement of a state before an intervention is applied. It does not mean that nothing is going on – in fact, during the baseline, a lot of confounding variables are in play, as well as a set of behaviours you might wish to change using an intervention. Baselines must be measured carefully to ensure that they are stable before proceeding with an intervention.

Next, you would consider introducing some kind of experimental manipulation, usually a treatment or intervention. This would be called, quite sensibly, B. Additional, different treatments or interventions take the remaining letters of the alphabet. Thus, a second treatment is C, then D, E, F and so on. Rarely would you find a single-case design that goes beyond a fifth or sixth intervention.

So, we can start to put these letters together into a design. The simplest design possible is A–B. In an A–B design, we measure our dependent variables at baseline, then we introduce a treatment and we look for its effect on the dependent variables during the B phase. That is it. However, you might spot a problem here. Sometimes things change without our doing anything. So, if we notice that a person who is obsessed with washing their hands stops washing their hands quite so much during the B phase, when we introduce a therapy, we cannot be sure the therapy was the reason. Therefore, we can adjust the design and we end up with the most common simple design, which is much better than the A-B: the A-B-A. By taking the treatment away again we can see if the unwanted hand-washing behaviour returns. If it does, then we can assume that the intervention was responsible for the reduction. We can bring in the element of assumed causality, essentially, which is a characteristic of experimental research.

Of course, there is something unethical about ending a trial on a non-treatment phase, so, in fact, we normally conduct A-B-A-B designs. Furthermore, if the unwanted behaviour appears both at baseline and the second A phase, and the drop in unwanted behaviour occurs in both B phases, we can be much more confident in the treatment applied.

Imagine what would happen if we wished to try out two different techniques to reduce compulsive hand-washing. Perhaps we have a talk therapy and a drug. We might then try the following types of design:

A-B-A-B-A-C-A-C-A
A-B-A-C-A-BC-A

In the second one, we actually try B and C separately first, then try them at the same time. That's why we depict it with the BC stuck together without a hyphen.

Primes

Sometimes, we might have varying amounts of an intervention or treatment. For example, we might wish to try out the effects of 10mg of a drug, stepping up to 15, 20 and so on. In this case, we cannot use different letters, because the intervention isn't different, there is simply more of it. For this, we use prime marks. Thus, 10mg of the drug might be B, but 15 would be B', 20 B" and 25 B''' and so on. Each little line is a prime. We would say 'B prime, B prime-prime or B prime-prime-prime', or we can say 'B prime, B double-prime and B triple-prime'. Therefore, we could have a design that was A-B-A-B'-B"-A or similar.

Practical application of single-case designs

Single-case designs are something of an historical oddity. They were very popular in the mid-twentieth century, used very regularly by the famous psychologist B. F. Skinner. They then fell out of usage for a while, but became popular again as clinical psychology and counselling literature grew in the 1970s onwards. Between 1939 and 1963, 246 single-case research articles had been published (Ittenbach & Lawhead, 1996), so it isn't a modern research method, but most university psychology departments still teach single-case designs only fleetingly.

Source: Ittenbach, R.F. & Lawhead, W. F. (1996). Historical and philosophical foundations of single-case research. In R. D. Franklin, D. B. Allison & B. S. Gorman (Eds.), *Design and analysis of single-case research*. Mahwah, NJ: Lawrence Erlbaum.

More complicated designs

Designs can be very complicated, as you will now realise. You can mix primes and letters with baselines and treatment removal phases in millions of combinations. There is no end to your creativity, but there are restrictions that would be brought about because your design might become impossible to carry out due to time or resource limitations.

Representing your data

In the case of most single-case designs, you represent your data in the form of raw scores plotted on a graph across time (across phases of the experiment) as in Figure 5.1. It really can be this simple. The reader can see at a glance what, if any, the effects of the intervention are.

The graphs can contain multiple dependent variables or even multiple participants if you have a single-case series design (see the next section). Just remember to keep the graphs simple. The more complicated everything gets, the less you remain faithful to the principles of single-case research.

Test your knowledge

5.1 Describe what happens in an A-B-A-C-A-BC-A design.

An answer to this question can be found on the companion website at: **www.pearsoned.co.uk/psychologyexpress**

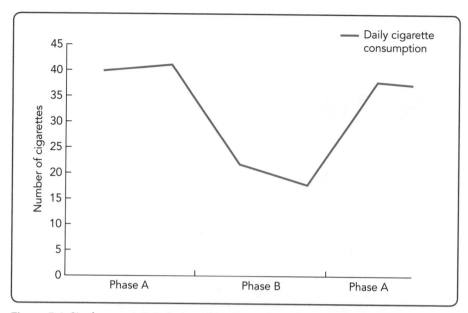

Figure 5.1 Single-case A-B-A design: the effect of an anti-smoking intervention

Single-case series designs

These are the simplest to explain, because they consist of single-case designs 'stuck together' as it were. Sometimes, you would prefer to demonstrate an intervention on a small group of people rather than on a single individual. This might be because you have access to that group or because you wish to show that your intervention works across a range of people. You might not have the luxury of running it with hundreds of people, which is resource-intensive and possibly unnecessary. Therefore, a single-case series design is a way of striking a deal between $N = 1$ and standard, larger-scale studies.

One type of single-case series design is the *crossover design*. Essentially, you might be worried about order effects in your research. To avoid this, randomly assign half of your participants to receive the treatments in one order, and the other half in reverse. Thus, for example, five people end up undergoing A-B-A-C-A and the other five A-C-A-B-A. You have a clear comparison between the two this way.

Obviously, there would reach a point perhaps when you have so many participants that it doesn't make sense to have a single-case series design because you have a number which could be subjected to statistical analysis. Depending on the nature of your design and the potential statistical analysis, the value of a single-case series design tends to peter out somewhere above 12 individuals. It is also not ethical to keep on conducting a study beyond where you have had the opportunity to 'prove your point'. This is something that applies to big, statistically analysed studies too. In the case of single-case research, we develop what we call 'stopping rules'. These are the equivalent of sample size calculations for larger studies.

CRITICAL FOCUS

Stopping rules

How might we create a set of stopping rules for a single-case series design? At what point might we decide to stop taking new participants into our study?

The things to think about fall into two main categories: ethical and methodological. Ethically, you should never make a study bigger than it needs to be. How big it needs to be, of course, is a methodological consideration, so that takes us full circle! You should never continue with a study where you discover an ethical problem. If someone is unexpectedly hurt or upset by a study and you have any reason to think that this could happen again, you stop. If you feel a study is showing nothing and that the picture is unlikely to change if you collect more data, then stop. This, of course, is a judgement call. In fact, the best way to handle these judgement calls is to have a small steering committee. You take your concerns to them and they decide, with you, whether to stop or not. That way, the responsibility is not left to one person, which can be dangerous in any circumstance in life.

Finally, if you feel that your study is showing dramatic, consistent results after just a few participants, take that to your steering group and they will probably order a stop. You can stop for good reasons, not just bad ones.

? Sample question   Problem-based learning

Read the research evidence on any topic of your choice. Then, set about deciding whether that evidence could be made stronger by the inclusion of single-case studies. Are single-case studies relevant for all areas of psychological inquiry?

Further reading Single-case and small-N research

Topic head	Key reading
Case studies	Bird, M., & Blair, A. (2007). Clinical psychology with complex presentations in old age, Nordic Psychology, 59, 59–74.
Single-case designs	Kazdin, A. E. (1982). Single-case research designs: Methods for clinical and applied settings. New York: Oxford University Press.
Single-case designs	Barlow, D. H. & Hersen, M. (1984). Single-case experimental designs (2nd Ed.). New York: Pergamon Press.
Single-case	Hilliard, R. B. (1993). Single-case methodology in psychotherapy process and outcome research. Journal of Consulting and Clinical Psychology, 61, 373–380.

Chapter summary – pulling it all together

→ Can you tick all the points from the revision checklist at the beginning of this chapter?

→ Attempt the sample question from the beginning of this chapter using the answer guidelines below.

→ Go to the companion website at **www.pearsoned.co.uk/psychologyexpress** to access more revision support online, including interactive quizzes, flashcards, You be the marker exercises as well as answer guidance for the Test your knowledge and Sample questions from this chapter.

Answer guidelines

 Sample question Essay

Using examples, show how single-case research can be experimental.

Approaching the question

Firstly, look carefully at the question and work out what is being asked for. The question asks only about single-case research, but that could include single-case series designs. It could also, theoretically, include case studies, which are not 'designs' but are a form of research, albeit not experimental. Examples are asked for. You'll also need to think about what 'experimental' means.

Important points to include

● Start with a paragraph alerting the reader to what you are going to discuss. This also tells them that you know what the question is about! Operationalise your definition of single-case research, showing what you wish to include in that definition and what you have decided does not fit.

● Then, lay out the defining characteristics of research that is experimental. Don't forget to make this literature-based, referring to textbooks where possible (since, in this case, textbooks rather than journal articles often are best). Talk about the scientific method and such matters as control, randomisation and cause and effect; don't forget to mention that statistics have got nothing to do with science or experimentation, even though people think they do. Single-case designs cannot be argued to be non-experimental because you do not normally analyse them statistically: that is a red herring.

● Choose two or three single-case research articles that show how the designs are used in practice and talk the reader through how they demonstrate experimental facets. Finally, summarise your position and leave a gem for the end. Perhaps mention, in your conclusion, the fact that single-case designs could even be said to pre-date the definition of experimentation itself, since they were used by the Ancient Greeks in their early explorations into human thought and behaviour.

Make your answer stand out

To make your answer stand out, you need to have read some interesting pieces of research using single-case methods. The essay marker is looking to discover things they didn't know about; no one wants their own lectures simply thrown back at them. There is not a lot of scope for being inventive in this essay, because most of it is factual, so good examples are your best chance.

Explore the accompanying website at www.pearsoned.co.uk/psychologyexpress

→ Prepare more effectively for exams and assignments using the answer guidelines for questions from this chapter.

→ Test your knowledge using multiple choice questions and flashcards.

→ Improve your essay skills by exploring the You be the marker exercises.

Notes

Observational methods

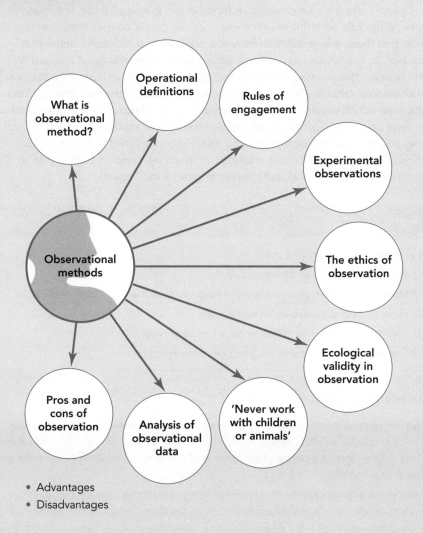

- Advantages
- Disadvantages

A printable version of this topic map is available from
www.pearsoned.co.uk/psychologyexpress

Introduction

Sometimes, the only way to find something out is to sit and watch. Not everything is amenable to experimentation. There are various phenomena that change massively when you try to investigate them using traditional experimental methods. For example, free-form children's play is best simply observed. Try to experiment with it and it becomes unnatural. Children play without any encouragement or interference from us, so often the best way to collect data on play is to observe it happening. Similarly, if you want to know how people use a traffic crossing or how people queue at a bar, it makes no sense to meddle with the environment: just watch. Of course, that doesn't mean that there are no rules to how you observe and it doesn't mean that observation cannot be used in conjunction with an experimental method. We still try to do things in a systematic and controlled way, with appropriate pre-set measurement criteria. Furthermore, observation can be the way of collecting data in an actual experiment too. Imagine I want to know whether a portrait of the boss on the wall affects how people interact in a staffroom. I can do this using an experimental design and the observation is how I collect my data. In this chapter, we will look at the ways in which we conduct both types of observation: experimental and non-experimental (or 'naturalistic').

> → **Revision checklist**
>
> *Essential points to revise are:*
> ❑ What observational designs look like
> ❑ How to set up an observational design so that it is valid and replicable
> ❑ How to define variables operationally
> ❑ The advantages and disadvantages of observation
> ❑ The ethical problems associated with observation

Assessment advice

- Observational method assessments normally either take the form of short-answer questions, including multiple choice, or more involved studies where you might design a piece of research and carry it out, analysing the data and writing a report.
- For short-answer questions, the main thing is that you understand the advantages and disadvantages of observational methods and know about the different types – for example, participant observation versus non-intrusive observation.

- For pieces of research, you need to bring all of your research and problem-solving skills to bear on the issue and approach the design of research in a logical, systematic way, looking for confounding variables and design flaws at every turn.

Sample question

Could you answer this question? Below is a typical essay question that could arise on this topic.

 Sample question *Essay*

Observation, as a method, is so flawed as to be useless. Discuss.

Guidelines on answering this question are included at the end of this chapter, whilst further guidance on tackling other exam questions can be found on the companion website at: **www.pearsoned.co.uk/psychologyexpress**

What is observational method?

In its simplest form, the observational method involves watching something, then writing down what happened. It is almost indistinguishable from journalism. It is free, but it isn't free from bias or prejudice. Whilst sometimes all you can do is watch and take note, that isn't necessarily good enough for the average psychologist, because we know just how selective and flawed observation and memory can be. We tend to want something more than 'the evidence of our senses'. The observational methods used by psychologists aim to be systematic, reliable and valid. These are our three key criteria that determine how we progress and prevent us from simply taking notes and passing them off as science, as it were. These three criteria all revolve around the idea that whatever we observe needs to be observed and observable by someone else, who would draw the same conclusions. We can, and should, help this along by recording our observations to play back later, but this in itself raises ethical issues. Interestingly enough, the media do not have the same things to worry about. They can film people, and do, all the time without needing to submit their ideas to an ethics committee. However, scientists must justify their work in a much more tightly controlled way. Therefore, observational method is sometimes very easy to conduct, but often difficult to get permission to carry out.

Observation is, arguably, not a method at all, but actually a technique. This is a subtle difference but an important one. The experimental method is a wide-ranging set of ways of collecting data based around the systematic manipulation of variables. Qualitative methods are ways of collecting data that are quite distinct in themselves. However, observation can be used to yield qualitative or quantitative data and can be nothing more than a way of measuring the dependent variable, even in a true experiment. This is what makes it a technique rather than a method.

Test your knowledge

6.1 Is observation a method or a technique of data collection?

6.2 What makes qualitative observation different from quantitative observation?

Answers to these questions can be found on the companion website at:
www.pearsoned.co.uk/psychologyexpress

Operational definitions

In order to run any observational study, you need to agree on operational definitions, especially in terms of observations being made. You can't simply tell someone to go to the park and 'note down any examples of children being aggressive to each other'. This yields more questions. If someone asked you to do this, you really would want to know more. What you would need is the information on *operational definitions*. Operational definitions are the meanings of certain things for the purposes of a study. It is not about the true meanings, per se, but what you have decided things mean in the rather restricted research you are conducting. Therefore, aggression can mean many things, and aggressive acts can take hundreds of forms, but to make a study simple and feasible we might decide that we are only counting blows using the fist or open hand to the body or face that cause the recipient to look shocked or upset. Of course, we would also need to define 'looks' of shock and upset, but we are narrowing things down to, for example, avoid 'play fighting' where children hit each other lightly and no injury or upset is caused or intended. In addition, we haven't even mentioned kicking, spitting, biting and a host of other possibilities. You can see how complicated even the simplest study quickly becomes.

Operational definitions are important because they mean that different observers know what they are looking for and they allow other people to try to replicate the study you have carried out. They help to make what you have done transparent to the outsider, but they also help you to remember what you did on day one so that you do not do something different on the second day of observation, which creates unnecessary 'noise' in your data.

Rules of engagement

The rules of engagement include operational definitions, but they also pertain to the what, where and when in data collection. These are often crucial to determine beforehand because they are usually needed by ethics committees who have to decide in advance whether or not your proposed research can go ahead.

What are you going to observe? Where are you going to observe it and when? These might seem simple, but they are not in reality. Firstly, you set your operational definitions, the 'what'. Imagine you have decided to study what causes people to press lift buttons repeatedly whilst waiting for a lift. We have all seen people turn up and keep pressing, even though the button is lit and the lift is coming (or so we believe). Perhaps you get annoyed when you have already pressed the button, but someone comes along and presses it too, almost as if they don't 'trust' that you have pressed it properly! Who does this? Is there a pattern to it? To keep it simple, we are going to work on the basis of style of dress. Our hypothesis is that people dressed casually will respond differently from those wearing formal dress, but we are not going to specify a direction. We don't know if wearing a suit makes people more or less likely to press the button repeatedly. We have also decided to only study the situation where a single person is waiting for the lift, not multiples. So, let us proceed. Each observer, if you have more than one, which you should, receives a sheet that defines the behaviour in question, rather like this.

- *Dependent variable observation*: repeated lift button pressing. Firstly, determine that the button is lit. Start the clock. Record the time from button press to lift arriving and mark out each subsequent button press in between. Exclude visually impaired people who might not see the light. Exclude people who re-press because the light goes out inexplicably without the lift arriving. This can happen where staff members in the lift override lift-calls when using the lift to urgently transport goods from floor to floor.

- *Independent variable observation*: each participant should be recorded for style of dress, in either 'casual', 'formal' or 'mixed' categories. 'Formal' is defined as a suit for men or women, including without tie for men. 'Mixed' would include a formal suit jacket with T-shirt and jeans, or a formal suit with training shoes, or a woman wearing a formal skirt with a casual T-shirt. Casual clothing includes all sportswear, cotton chinos, clothing with slogans or large designer logos, baseball caps, non-formal shirts, such as those with checked patterns, worn inside or outside the trousers. When it is difficult to determine which of the three categories is to be applied, discard the observation.

- *Sites of observation*: Two lifts are to be observed in the Fandango Hotel, San Pedro. The two lifts furnish the north and east entrances to the hotel. Observations are to take place at busy times, determined by the hotel to be 8am to 10am and 4pm to 10pm.

Can you see what has been done here? Although you can argue with the researchers about the decisions they have made, at the very least the decisions are explicit, transparent and reproducible. They are open to question precisely because they are clear and written down. When you are designing an observational study, try to think of every detail. Furthermore, it is important to run a pilot study. This will allow you to make note of things that happen which you might not have predicted (changes in behaviour that occur linked to daily patterns associated with any number of variables such as time of day, weather, light and so on) and it will give you a sense of how easy your protocols and operational definitions are to follow and work with. If your researchers or observers are going to discover all sorts of problems collecting data, it is always better to find that out before the main study starts.

Test your knowledge

6.3 What questions should you ask yourself when designing an observational study? How can you ensure that you capture all of the behaviours you are studying?

An answer to this question can be found on the companion website at: **www.pearsoned.co.uk/psychologyexpress**

Experimental observations

When observation takes place within a setting where we have manipulated a variable, we end up with what is, in essence, an experimental design. Therefore, it isn't the case that all observation is somehow wishy-washy and hard to draw conclusions from. If you set up an experiment to find out how people behave in a particular situation, and you manipulate the situation, then as long as everything else stays the same you can assume that your independent variable caused any fluctuation in behaviour. It isn't the observational data collection process that determines whether you have an experiment or not, but the design of your study. The simplest observational designs might be those involving a single, clear, two-level independent variable, such as determining how long male children play with an object coloured blue or pink. You simply try out children with either the pink or the blue toy. If you wish to see if you get a different pattern of behaviour with girls and boys, you would introduce a second independent variable and you suddenly have a 2×2 study. In these cases, you would need to define 'playing with' the toy, then measure both time spent per discrete episode of play and number of episodes. This is important because you might find that there is no difference between pink and blue in total time spent, but there is a difference in number of episodes of play. It might be crucial to know if play was made up of ten episodes of two minutes or two episodes of ten minutes.

However, this study is only quasi-experimental, because we cannot make the children male or female, so one of our variables is predetermined and not by us but by nature. We can carry out observational studies that are entirely experimental, though. For example, we want to see if we can increase the number of times people use the stairs, instead of the lifts, at their place of work. We spend a week observing stair usage, then we send people a message about using the stairs with their payslips. Then we turn up again, for an equivalent amount of time, and observe stair use after the payslip intervention. If we see an increase of stair usage, we assume it was caused by our intervention. This is an experimental study using observational data as our dependent variable.

KEY STUDY

What makes a good observer?

Allport (1937) wrote a classic book on personality that contains a discussion about what makes a good observer. His criteria are interesting because they give us an insight into the way of thinking of early psychologists, even though we may disagree today. According to Allport, there are eight key skills of an observer.

1 *Experience*: Allport claims that you need to be more than 30 years old to be a good observer.

2 *Similarity*: when the observer has things in common with the observed, the data are better.

3 *Intelligence*: this refers in particular to being able to figure out the relationship between cause and effect.

4 *Insight*: this is in relation to understanding that as an observer you have an effect on your surroundings and those you observe.

5 *Complexity*: it is easier to observe something simpler than yourself.

6 *Detachment*: good observers don't get involved.

7 *Aesthetic attitude*: the best observers appreciate what they are observing and enjoy what they do.

8 *Social intelligence*: this refers to the ability of the observer to discern what is going on in social situations. Therefore, a good observer would be intuitive and sensitive to others' moods and feelings and the social dynamics between people.

Do you agree with Allport? Can you think of other characteristics to add to the list or would you say that any of the above are irrelevant?

Source: Allport, G. W. (1937). Personality. New York: Holt.

The ethics of observation

As you might imagine, observational studies are prone to generating all sorts of ethical dilemmas. You can't just watch people and assume it's OK to do it. The first problem we have is whether it is OK to do things without the consent of your 'participants'. Collecting data from people without their knowing could be seen to be unethical, even when you are simply observing them doing what they would normally do, in a public place.

If you need to store your data, you raise new ethical questions. Filming people without their knowledge is, in some situations, illegal, regardless of whether it is ethical. Modern data protection legislation has, some would argue, 'killed' old-fashioned observational studies, since it is very difficult to conduct any surreptitious or clandestine recording of people, especially children, for example.

If you intend carrying out observational work, ask yourself the following ethical questions.

● Will my participants be inconvenienced in any way?
● Will my data collection result in my having information about individuals who are identifiable by image if not by name?
● How will I store data?
● Is there a way of obtaining consent?
● Would the people being observed be likely to be upset or annoyed if they knew about the study?
● In the case of participant observation, in particular, would the researchers be in any danger?

Ecological validity in observation

Elsewhere in this book we discuss the issue of ecological validity and how it is often misunderstood as a concept. It is often assumed that experimental, laboratory-based studies are not ecologically valid, because some people mistakenly think that ecological validity cannot apply in a laboratory situation, when, in fact, it can if the findings from the laboratory can be legitimately applied to a naturalistic setting. However, we should apply a critical eye to observational studies in the other direction too. Some people also fall into the trap of believing that all studies carried out outside the laboratory are ecologically valid. This is just as erroneous. Not all studies that involve observation are equal in terms of potential ecological validity. This might seem odd, but you have to think about the very nature of conducting field studies. Particant observation is always compromised in ecological validity, because you cannot be sure that what you observe would happen without you there. Thus, the world with you taking part in it is quite similar to a laboratory you work in: rather artificial. Any form of obstrusive observation, where you could be spotted with your notepad or camera suffers in the same way. However, even the most unobtrusive observation can lack ecological validity on a very subtle level, because you choose what to observe and what to ignore. There is no bigger picture and that means the complicated world is simplified. The act of studying *one* aspect of the multivariate environment or behaviour reduces the ecological validity of your findings.

 Sample question *Problem-based learning*

Imagine that you have been asked to develop a protocol for an observational study into the food-seeking behaviour of rats. Would it be best to conduct this in the wild or in a laboratory situation? Does it matter?

'Never work with children or animals'

This old phrase has particular resonance for a discussion of observation methods, because they are the most pertinent methods to use for many studies with children, especially those in their first months of life, and are probably the only methods of gathering data from animals. You cannot ask an animal what it is thinking or why it is behaving a certain way. All you can do is watch and make note of patterns of behaviour. Whilst it is probably unfair to suggest that one should not work with children or animals, it is certainly the case that there are limits to the work you can do with them. Observational data collection is crucial in these populations.

Make your answer stand out

If you are asked to write an essay on observational methods, the immediately obvious thing to do is find studies in classic areas where observation is used, particularly in child development. Consider thinking outside of the box and looking instead at, for example, animal behaviour. The majority of work in comparative psychology and ethology is observational, for example. It might be much more interesting to the reader if you discuss the use of observation in studies of garden snail behaviours than in schoolchildren... Just remember that there needs to be psychology in there, so don't get too carried away.

Analysis of observational data

Observational data can be analysed in a number of ways, ranging from the qualitative to the hard-line quantitative. However, the most important thing is that we can demonstrate that observers can be trusted. This is achieved by attempting to put a figure on the agreement of two raters. We call this, in statistical terms, a coefficient of concordance, of which the most common is Cohen's kappa. When we have observations that are essentially quantitative in nature, such as the number of times a child drops a teddy bear or the number of times someone smiles, we can use kappa to see how the raters or observers agree. However, it doesn't work for every type of observation, especially those that are more qualitative, or journalistic, in nature. As for participant observation, you would need to send two researchers out into the field, under cover, as it were! That would be a tricky act to pull off, not to mention twice as worrying, ethically.

Of course, in theory, data collected by observation can be analysed in just about any way that is appropriate, both qualitative and quantitative, and with a range of analysis methods, statistical or otherwise. However, when the data collected from observations are quantitative in nature (the number of times things happen, for example), then we are quite likely to use chi-squared or some kind of correlation to analyse the data. Correlations are particularly important in *epidemiological observational studies*. What are these? Well, imagine if we wish to collect routine medical data and then look for relationships in the data. Perhaps we are interested in knowing if daily fruit and vegetable consumption is linked to bowel cancer rates. Both of these are variables we effectively 'observe' in our sample; we don't interfere or try to make them happen. This is a rather technical use of the term 'observation' but nevertheless you should be aware of it. In this case, correlation would be entirely appropriate as a method of statistical analysis.

Key term

It might seem rather obvious at first glance, but **data** can take many forms and we should be aware of them. Holliday (2007) lists various types of data in qualitative studies: descriptions of behaviour, of events, of institutions, of appearances, personal narratives, talk, visual records and documents of all types. In quantitative terms, observational data can technically take the form of *any* of these, but will be converted in some way to some kind of numerical measure, such as the number of times a particular event occurs, rather than a description of it.

Longitudinal observation

Beelman and Schmidt-Denter (2009) conducted a longitudinal observational study of mother–child interaction after parental separation. In a very large study, they compared interactions between mother and child in 60 dyads, 10, 25 and 40 months after the mother and father separated, with interactions in dyads where no such separation had occurred. The sheer amount of work involved in the study is impressive. They discovered, through a statistical analysis of certain behaviours that were videotaped, when mothers were separated from fathers due to divorce, for example, the mothers display less empathy and support for the children. Naturally, this is a study with a very strong political dimension to it and some of the findings could be used by conservative commentators to criticise separation because of its apparent effects on the family. However, the authors point out that two years after divorce the effects disappear. This shows why longitudinal aspects should be considered in research, although they are often neglected in observational work, which is commonly cross-sectional only in nature.

Source: Beelman, W., & Schmidt-Denter, U. (2009). Mother–child interaction following marital separation: A longitudinal observation study. *European Psychologist, 14*, 307–319.

Pros and cons of observation

Observations, like any data collection methods, have their good points and their drawbacks.

Advantages

- Observational studies can be cheap, in that often no materials or apparatus need to be bought.
- Observational studies can save you time on consent, participant information sheets, debriefing and other things normally associated with research studies.
- You get to observe things as they happen, with usually little chance that you are affecting the outcome.
- If you film behaviours for repeated viewing, observational studies can allow for revisiting the data many times to look for new aspects, potentially deriving maximum value from the data.

Disadvantages

- Observational studies can take a very long time to carry out. This is especially the case when you are studying rare behaviours. If something doesn't happen very often, you have to wait for what could be months before you see it.
- Observational studies can be expensive, especially if labour costs need to be high to capture rare behaviours.

- Observational studies can be difficult to justify or conduct, ethically.
- Observational studies can be complicated in terms of defining the behaviours under study. You might miss the most important things while you are looking at something else.
- You can never be sure if you are seeing what you think you are.
- You can only imply causality in observational studies carried out with experimental manipulation of the environment.

CRITICAL FOCUS

Participant observation

Participant observation is a specific type of observation that very few psychologists use, but that has been a mainstay of some of the most famous studies in sociology. Exactly as it sounds, participant observation is an unstructured method that requires the researcher to participate in the behaviour being observed. It is rather like working 'under cover', as the police or journalists often do. You join a group of people and do what they do, in order to discover what life is like for them. As you would imagine, this is an exciting and fascinating way to study behaviour and you can find things out that otherwise would remain hidden, but it is heavily flawed and unethical, so is seldom used any more. Covert participant observation is unethical because the people do not know that they are being studied and they do not know your true identity as a researcher. Whilst this might be acceptable for the purposes of national security, it simply is not for research. Furthermore, just because you are researching under cover does not mean that the behaviour you observe is normal. You are a participant, which means your own actions change what happens. No matter how much you try to behave normally, your very presence alters the dynamic. Therefore, there is no reason to assume you are getting data and information that are reliable.

It is possible to declare your identity upfront and remove the ethical problem entirely, but this is almost certain to create more 'noise' or 'error' in your observations, since people know there is an outsider in their ranks. There is, therefore, somewhat limited value in turning up and saying 'Hello. I am a researcher, here to study what your lives are like. Please carry on as normal.'

One fairly normal participant observation that can work is where you are studying children in Piagetian-style tasks. Such tasks typically require you to undertake a task with the child, asking questions as you go along. Although the questions are mostly set in advance, there has to be scope for improvisation because there are elements of unpredictability in the tasks (not to mention working with children!). When you set up a conservation task, for example, everyone knows you are a researcher, but the meaning of this is somewhat lost on the average small child anyway. You engage with the child, asking questions. The child commonly thinks of you as 'teacher' or 'friend to play with'. As such, you become both an observer and a participant, without any significant ethical problems.

CRITICAL FOCUS

Practical application of concepts

Observational techniques can be used in a wide variety of ways. Macintosh and Dissanayake (2006) used observation to make comparisons between children with Asperger syndrome (AS) and those with high-functioning autism (HFA). An observer watched children playing and interacting, including a normally developing control group of children. Different types of play were observed and categorised: of particular interest was social versus non-social play, since, of course, people with autism tend to have difficulties in social relationships. Although the normally developing children were more engaged in social interaction than either of the other two groups, differences were observed between the AS children and those with HFA. AS children spent much more of their time in conversation than HFA children, but no other play-related differences were observed. The results help to show that autism and AS are distinct from each other in the behavioural patterns associated with them. Methodologically the study was interesting because the observer did not know what the diagnosis was for each child they were observing. Why is that important for this design?

Source: Macintosh, K., & Dissanayake, C. (2006). A comparative study of the spontaneous social interactions of children with high-functioning autism and children with Asperger's disorder. *Autism*, 10(2), 199–220.

Further reading Observational studies

Topic	Key reading
Participant observation: this is a fascinating study where the researcher pretended to be a patient in a rehabilitation hospital (note that this would no longer be possible because of ethical concerns)	French, D. J., McDowell, R. E., & Keith, R. A. (1972). Participant observation as a patient in a rehabilitation hospital. *Rehabilitation Psychology, 19*, 89–95.
Observations of animal species: an important paper for understanding why observation is crucial for cross-species research	Russon, A. E., Kuncoro, P., Ferisa, A., & Handayani, D. P. (2010). How orangutans (Pongo pygmaeus) innovate for water. *Journal of Comparative Psychology, 124*, 14–28.

? *Sample question*   *Assessment*

You have been tasked with developing a protocol for an observational study. You have five researchers, all of whom need to be sent to various locations to observe behaviour. You are to produce their instructions. They must know exactly what to do, and when and where to do it. The behaviour you are researching is 'helping' in supermarket carparks. The independent variables are sex of the person helped and sex of the helper. Naturally, you will need to pay a lot of attention to the meaning of 'helping behaviour'.

Chapter summary – pulling it all together

→ Can you tick all the points from the revision checklist at the beginning of this chapter?

→ Attempt the sample question from the beginning of this chapter using the answer guidelines below.

→ Go to the companion website at www.pearsoned.co.uk/psychologyexpress to access more revision support online, including interactive quizzes, flashcards, You be the marker exercises as well as answer guidance for the Test your knowledge and Sample questions from this chapter.

Further reading for Chapter 6

Topic	Key reading
Skills for observation	Boice, R. (1983). Observational skills. *Psychological Bulletin, 93*, 3–29.

Answer guidelines

 Sample question   *Essay*

Observation, as a method, is so flawed as to be useless. Discuss.

Approaching the question

Your first step is to think about the statement and how you will break it down into its essential components. The statement is very extreme, so you might wish to point that out. Make a list of the good and bad sides to observational research, since that is essentially what the question boils down to. You have very little constraint in how you could approach this, since the only command in the title is to 'discuss' the statement. How you discuss it is mostly up to you.

Important points to include

● Begin with a general statement, perhaps pointing out that all methods have their advantages and disadvantages, including the most stringent. Perhaps give an example of how, for instance, something like a controlled experiment doesn't necessarily give you rich data on how your participants think, just how they behave.

● Then, work your way through the disadvantages of various types of observation, then the advantages. Then, weigh up one set of comments against the other. Then, make your reasoned judgement, comparing it with the statement in the question.

- After that, discuss how the suggestion that observation is useless is extreme and all things have their values. Point out that sometimes observation is all we have and give an example.

Make your answer stand out

The best answers to this question would be those where the student sees a new angle, as is the case with any assessment. In short, question the question. What does observational method mean? What does useless mean? A lot depends on how you define those when tackling the question. There is a challengeable presupposition in most questions and do not be afraid to tear questions apart.

Explore the accompanying website at www.pearsoned.co.uk/psychologyexpress

→ Prepare more effectively for exams and assignments using the answer guidelines for questions from this chapter.
→ Test your knowledge using multiple choice questions and flashcards.
→ Improve your essay skills by exploring the You be the marker exercises.

Notes

Notes

Measuring attitudes

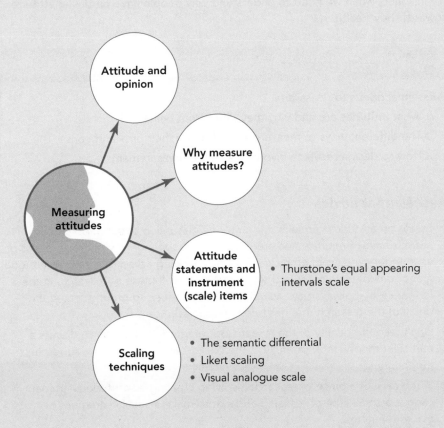

- Attitude and opinion
- Measuring attitudes
- Why measure attitudes?
- Attitude statements and instrument (scale) items
  - Thurstone's equal appearing intervals scale
- Scaling techniques
  - The semantic differential
  - Likert scaling
  - Visual analogue scale

A printable version of this topic map is available from
www.pearsoned.co.uk/psychologyexpress

Introduction

In psychology, we have a special name for points of view: we call them *attitudes*. Attitudes are different from beliefs. You can have a belief and an attitude on a subject. An atheist might say that religious people are wrong. That would be a belief. However, she might also say that religious people deserve to have a right to free expression and are as important as everyone else. That is her *attitude*. Similarly, you can *believe* that the Loch Ness monster exists, but have an *attitude* of indifference towards it. Indeed, any combination of beliefs and attitudes is possible. Sometimes psychologists need to find out what people's attitudes are and the measurement of attitudes is essential for a large body of work in social psychology, not to mention other areas of our discipline – for instance, when we need to understand why people have particular attitudes towards their health.

 Revision checklist

Essential points to revise are:

- ❑ What attitudes are and why they differ from beliefs
- ❑ The different ways to measure attitudes and their pros and cons
- ❑ How to design research involving attitude measurement

Assessment advice

- Essays on attitudes can take the form of a discussion of social psychology areas, such as prejudice and stereotyping, or, commonly, you are assessed on your understanding of attitude surveying by being asked to create an attitude measurement instrument and test it out as a 'real' piece of research. In the former case, it always pays, when discussing theory, to ground that in the detail of the research that has been conducted.

- Don't take the quality of the research for granted. If you wish to discuss a particular theory, look carefully at the background research that supports the theory.

- In the case of a piece of research involving creating an attitude instrument, choose a small area of research and aim to make a small instrument of five to ten items.

- Doing a little piece of work well is always better than tackling something too large and biting off more than you can chew. This commonly leads to problems.

Sample question

Could you answer this question? Below is a typical essay question that could arise on this topic.

 Sample question   *Essay*

Discuss, with examples from the research literature, the notion that attitude measurement is as scientific as any other branch of psychology.

Guidelines on answering this question are included at the end of this chapter, whilst further guidance on tackling other exam questions can be found on the companion website at: **www.pearsoned.co.uk/psychologyexpress**

Attitude and opinion

Key terms

You might wonder what the difference is between **attitude** and **opinion**. Well, most of the time you will see them used as if they were the same, but for those who do make a distinction it is as follows. As McNemar (1946) states, attitudes are invisible. They are a theoretical stance towards a particular subject. When someone expresses an attitude, in speech or writing, that is an opinion. So, our attitude surveys are actually opinion surveys, because that's the data we collect, but because we collect a number of opinions around a construct, we call it an attitude survey. The difference is subtle, but nevertheless exists.

Often, psychologists are interested in modelling attitudes, so that they are predictable. Attitude formation has fascinated us for decades and a lot of work has been directed at figuring out why we have the attitudes that we do and, more importantly, how they can change or be changed over time. When politicians talk about winning people over, they essentially are talking about changing their attitudes. Advertisements are another kind of 'attitude engineering' in action. Why do companies advertise their products? It isn't just to tell you that they exist. If that were the case, all advertisements would be identical. Advertisements try to persuade you that the product in question is worth having; that is, the manufacturer wants to shape your attitude towards the product in a positive way.

Why measure attitudes?

Just as in observation, sometimes the only way to discover something is to do the obvious. Sometimes we have to observe and sometimes we have to ask questions. Measuring attitudes is a way of asking questions, although, ironically, we normally assess attitudes not by using questions, but by using statements which a person can agree or disagree with. We'll come to that in more detail later.

You can't access attitudes by observation without incurring a whole host of problems. It *is* vaguely possible, but usually never worth doing. For example, if I start talking about whelks and you grimace and squirm, I would naturally assume that you don't like whelks. It is an assumption, but a reasonable one. However, that's all I can work out from this situation. Let us take something more subtle. Sometimes, because of all sorts of pressures from society and the like, people might hide their attitudes. When you talk about a subject, they might not give away their attitude. For example, even people who hold racist views will often keep them to themselves unless they know that the company they are in allows them to express them. If I were to speak to a racist person about how much I love travel, meeting wonderful people from all over the world, how much I value different people and so on, I might not be challenged at all. This would be especially true if there were ten people saying the same thing as me and he or she was the only person who disagreed. Social pressure would suppress the attitude. However, the attitude is still present. Attitude measurement instruments are used to discover those attitudes. By presenting people with carefully constructed statements to agree or disagree with, confidentially or usually anonymously, with no possibility of social pressure or need for conformity, we can really ascertain what people actually think. There really is no other way.

Key terms

Scale, scale and instrument: You might have had a double-take when reading the title of this box. Yes, we really did mean to state 'scale' twice. Unfortunately, the word 'scale' gets used in two different ways... and you need to be aware of this before you read on, especially when reading other books and articles that won't point out this distinction. Scale is often used to mean the whole thing that you give to people – for example, a *stress scale*. This is synonymous with 'instrument' or 'test'. However, when you respond to an item within a scale, you do so using a scale (such as a Likert scale or a visual analogue scale). Yes, it seems quite strange, but it is true.

We prefer to use the terms 'instrument', 'item' and 'scale', because that prevents confusion. After all, a scale is a thing you use to measure with, not the thing itself. You select some grapes and each individual one is a grape. Together, you have a bunch of grapes. To know what weight of grapes you have, you put them on a scale or a pair of scales. This measures their value as it were. You don't put 'a scale of grapes' on a scale, but that is exactly analogous to the way in which these terms are used in psychometrics, unfortunately.

Attitude statements and instrument (scale) items

In order to measure attitudes using an attitude instrument we need to start with an idea of what it is we hope to measure. This is something students often struggle with. Keep it simple, always, and make sure that your items match the overall construct you are measuring.

What is a construct? Well, it is essentially something you wish to measure. It is an overarching issue or concept or category of things. Race is a construct, which is why it doesn't sound odd to say that you are hoping to measure attitudes to race. So are love, education and so on. In fact, most things can be constructs, including naturally occurring objects and phenomena like rain or mountains. Start with your construct, then you need to think about how to create statements relevant to that construct.

Often, these statements are derived from research involving discussions, between the researchers or sometimes the general public, on the topic. Even the simplest things people say can be used as attitude statements, such as 'I don't like rain'. You collect these, mix them up and, to avoid acquiescence response bias, you make sure you have some items that 'point' the other way. For example, if you have 'I don't like rain', there should be a 'matching' item such as 'I enjoy it when it rains'.

Key term

Acquiescence response bias is the name we use to describe the phenomenon where people answering questions, either orally or on paper, get into a habit of saying the same thing over and over again and switch off from thinking about what they are hearing or reading. It can ruin a questionnaire if the questions or items become seemingly predictable.

There are some old practical jokes that demonstrate a kind of acquiescence response bias. For example, you might have come across the one about cows. You ask someone the following questions, waiting for the answer each time.

'What is white, comes in bottles and rhymes with silk?'

'What do you put on breakfast cereal?'

'What comes from the breasts of a mammal?'

'What do cows drink?'

Naturally, the person tends to respond to each question with the word 'milk' even though cows tend to drink water, although their calves drink milk for some months in the early part of their lives.

This is acquiescence response bias in action. It is a bad thing for us because, although people are prone to it naturally, it reveals a kind of cognitive laziness that can ruin our data. By mixing the items up so that sometimes the left-hand side of the scale means you agree, but sometimes the right-hand side means you agree, people have to read each item carefully and consider the scale before responding.

You can test for acquiescence response bias in your data by looking at the answers people have given you to items that are essentially identical apart from the direction they are 'facing'. If someone says that they love cheese on one item and then says they hate cheese further down in the questionnaire, you can assume they have not read the questions properly. This means that it might be safer to ignore all of their data, excluding them from the study. You can't just choose what you think they wanted to say…

You should pay particular attention to repetition in your items, remembering that in the early stages of instrument construction you need to have similar items, but not obvious repetitions or items so similar that your respondents become frustrated. Start with around two or three times more items than you intend using in the final version. You will lose some later, when you have performed various actions to reduce them down.

Think also about avoiding items that are likely to be useless because they are too extreme. If you have items like 'I always go out when it rains', almost every single person would have to disagree. Sometimes it rains when you are asleep, for instance. No matter how much you like rain, it would be hard to go out every time it happens. 'I like to go out when it rains' is a much more sensible suggestion for an item measuring that element of attitude to rain.

Avoid items that are ambiguous or double-barrelled. A double-barrelled item is one that has two statements stuck together, so the person responding isn't sure what they are responding to and so you aren't either when you get the data. For example, an item like 'I love rain and wish it always was raining' contains two assertions. It is possible to love rain without wishing it was always raining. It is also possible to wish it was always raining without saying you love it. Finally, it is also possible to agree to both. So, when you get your data, how do you know what your respondent was thinking when they answered that item? Most double-barrelled items can be corrected by creating two separate items from each one. Ambiguous items are to be avoided for similar reasons: for example, 'Rain takes my breath away'. Whilst for most people this could be likely to mean something like 'rain amazes me', some people might literally become breathless in the rain, just like they often do on windy days. Thus, their response to an item like this doesn't tell us about their *attitude*.

Avoid also unnecessarily complicated or unusually worded items or slang. This would include double-negatives, such as 'I wouldn't want to not ignore someone.' Sometimes, if you look at older instruments, you will find items that contain words not commonly used any more, like 'pep' (meaning 'energy' or 'vigour'). It is always surprising to see these instruments still being used in research today. Languages change in many ways over time and to pretend that isn't happening is a recipe for disaster. One famous scale for measuring pain uses the word 'lancinating', which many people simply don't ever use or understand.

The practical application of attitude measurement

It is easy to think that attitude measurement is all about discovering what attitudes people have, in order to develop theories about how those attitudes form. However, whilst that is what social psychologists tend to do, it isn't the whole story. There are practical uses for attitude surveys, without a need to develop any theories. Two main practical applications of attitude surveying come in trying to understand what customers think, or what staff themselves think, about a company or service. Customers can include hospital patients or car buyer or just about anybody, and staff can include anyone who deals with those clients or customers. Consultants often spend their time surveying attitudes in an organisation in order to know what is felt by those involved, usually with the aim to change things in order to put right any negative attitudes that are held.

Thurstone's equal appearing intervals scale

Thurstone (Thurstone & Chave, 1929) developed a number of methods of scaling and was largely interested in the selection of the items to be used rather than the scale per se. There is an argument that the scale is less important than items carefully chosen to reflect opinions with a broad spread across a construct. Therefore, although Thurstone's work is referred to as scaling, it is technically more about instrument construction than scale construction.

In Thurstone's method, you have to begin with a very large number of items for inclusion. Even if you only want about 12 in the final instrument, you need to start with around 100. You then get people to sift through the items, each being given a rating from 1 to 11. The rating is given on the basis of how favourable the item is to the construct. It therefore involves being very clear about the construct. For example, the construct might be something like **Being favourable towards marriage**. The participants in this stage are *not* giving their own attitudes. That comes much later, when you have your instrument constructed. Their task at this point is merely to rate each statement as to how much that statement is reflecting favourability towards marriage. That's what the 1–11 scale is for.

Eventually, you end up with items in categories or piles. The aim is to select items that are consistently found in each pile, as it were. So, if a particular statement is found spread across all the ratings, it is useless. If it is found spread across five ratings, perhaps 1, 2, 3, 4 and 5, then it is also not particularly useful and will probably also be lost. However, if every single person rates an item as a 7, then that is likely to become an item you use because it is 'sensitive' to detecting attitudes around that mark. Eventually, you have a set of items that should, in theory, detect attitudes across the entire range of possibilities, with little or no ambiguity.

Sample question   *Assessment*

Try out the initial stage of the development of an equal appearing intervals scale. Start with a construct, let us say 'attitudes to modern technology', and then try to create 100 items that might be used. What problems do you encounter?

Test your knowledge

7.1 What are the two meanings of 'scale' and how can they be confused?

An answer to this question can be found on the companion website at: **www.pearsoned.co.uk/psychologyexpress**

Scaling techniques

Attitude scaling is the term we use to describe the ways in which we judge attitudes. It is relatively easy to construct attitude statements, but harder to measure attitudes against them properly. There are several scaling methods, but the most common ones are described here.

The semantic differential

Developed by Osgood, Suci and Tannenbaum (1957), this is based upon asking people to respond showing how strong their feeling is on a scale ranging from one of a pair of bipolar opposites to another. For example:

Children should be seen and not heard. This comment is:

Good ———————————————————————— Bad

The respondent marks where on the line they feel their strength of feeling is best reflected. You can even do this with one construct and a set of words. For example:

Discrimination is:

Good ——————————————————— Bad

Strong ——————————————————— Weak

Unreasonable ——————————————— Reasonable

and so on. However, as you can see, this is a slightly odd way of scaling attitudes and does not tend to be used very often.

Likert scaling

This is the form of scaling that you will be most familiar with and, for the majority of instruments, this is the best compromise between ease of understanding for your respondents and quality of data you derive from it.

Likert (1932) created this form of scaling, which identifies fixed points along a dimension of extremes of agreement with a statement. Technically, it is possible to have a two-point Likert scale, consisting entirely of 'agree' and 'disagree', but this is hardly ever used because it simply isn't sensitive enough to pick up the wider range of opinions people tend to have. Similarly, most researchers would never use a three-point scale. Given that it is important to have a mid-point, this tends to mean that almost all Likert scales have odd numbers of points in them. Furthermore, in balancing out the need for a wide range against ease of response, something like 90 per cent of all Likert scales have either 5 or 7 points in them.

This is an example of a five-point response scale for an item.

Travel broadens the mind.

Disagree strongly	Disagree	Neither agree nor disagree	Agree	Agree strongly

Each point is labelled, which is intended to reduce ambiguity. The respondent is given as much information as possible in order to make a choice. Seven-point scales feature an additional two items in the range, of course.

Strongly disagree	Disagree	Disagree slightly	Neither agree nor disagree	Agree slightly	Agree	Strongly agree

> **? Sample question** *Problem-based learning*
>
> Your task is to try to develop an *11*-point Likert scale, for the following item:
>
> I always try to do my best.
>
> Remember that you must label each point on the scale. Reflect on the problems you encounter.

So, in short, the majority of attitude work we do involves Likert scales. Does that mean they are without problems? Well, no. Likert scales suffer from the difficulties you might have encountered when using them yourself in filling in questionnaires. Sometimes, you would like to give an answer that has not been made available to you. On a five-point Likert scale, it is quite easy to end up wishing it was a seven-point scale because your strength of opinion genuinely falls between two of the options. This becomes less of a problem with seven-point scales and almost disappears entirely with nine-point scales, but unfortunately we often struggle to find words to label the points on nine-point Likert scales!

Another problem is that the data from Likert scales can be misconstrued and misanalysed. Technically, the data are ordinal, but are often treated like interval data. Try as you might, you cannot be sure the difference between any two adjacent points on your scale is the same distance as that between any two other adjacent ones. For example, you cannot guarantee that all respondents agree that 'slightly disagree' to 'disagree' is the same distance as between 'slightly agree' and 'neither agree nor disagree'. Arguably, the mid-point is not in the middle at all; some people claim it is not even on the scale. So, the value of these scales is debatable, despite what some researchers would claim.

Yet another difficulty we find with Likert scaling, but not exclusively so, is that of response attenuation. The further we extend our scale, the fewer points on the scale are chosen by our respondents. This means that, even though we have seven points on the scale, for example, for various reasons people often choose their responses around a certain end of the scale or they are bunched up in the middle. The extremes at either end might be ignored completely or, depending on the nature of the item, they might be used exclusively. Imagine you had an item like:

Everyone should be drunk all of the time.

Very, very few people would agree with that statement. In fact, almost everyone would strongly disagree. That is attenuation in action. Naturally, well-chosen items that do not purvey extreme opinions should be used, in conjunction with our Likert scale, to avoid this scenario, although it still occurs.

Finally, Likert scales, and some others, can be criticised because they contain a neutral mid-point that some respondents confuse with 'don't know'. Now, of course, 'neither agree nor disagree' is not the same as 'don't know', but if *some* people would confuse them, we have a problem. Raaijmakers, Van Hoof, 't Hart, Verbogt and Vollebergh (2000) suggest that our scales should feature a separate 'don't know' to make it clear to respondents.

KEY STUDY

The work behind a scale

Wood et al. (2010) describe the development and use of a scale to measure attitudes towards God, the ATGS-9. They carried out a total of six studies to create appropriate items for the scale and to test those items out in terms of the crucial factors, such as face and construct validity, internal consistency, factor structure, temporal reliability and discriminant validity. The research shows just how much work goes into a scale that eventually contains just nine items. Eventually, the final, usable scale contained two 'subscales' that measure positive attitudes towards God and disappointment and anger with God. The researchers point out that the scale could have use when trying to put someone's spiritual or religious feelings into the context of any counselling or therapy they might be undergoing or vice versa. The authors give norms for different ethnic and religious groups, men and women and various ages. Regardless of the actual content of the work, a reading of this article demonstrates how good research is often like cooking. Lots of ingredients might be mixed together and simmered into a reduction that doesn't seem like very much but takes a lot of skill. Just because a final scale contains nine items doesn't mean you can create your own in five minutes. Sometimes things that appear simple are actually very complicated.

The visual analogue scale

This is essentially a version of the Likert scale, but, instead of fixed points on a scale, you have a continuous line and the respondent can therefore mark any point from, for instance, zero to ten centimetres. What this really gives us is marks on a scale of 100 instead of maybe 5 or 7. It makes analysis relatively easy because all your numbers are on this scale from 0 to 100, which you can ascertain using a plastic ruler laid on the questionnaire! You can then, some argue, treat the data like ratio data. Some argue that you cannot, however, and this is simply making the data look as if they were ratio when they were not. After all, it is very difficult to argue that 25 mm for one participant means the same as 25 mm for another... Most of the time, using a Likert scale with a good number of fixed points is a safer bet, less prone to criticism because 'what you see is what you get'.

Test your knowledge

7.2 What are the advantages and disadvantages of Likert and visual analogue scales?

7.3 Why does semantic differential scaling not work well for most psychological research?

Answers to these questions can be found on the companion website at: **www.pearsoned.co.uk/psychologyexpress**

? Sample question   Essay

What should a researcher consider when developing an attitude measurement instrument?

CRITICAL FOCUS

Attitude consistency

Sometimes work on the theories of attitude formation isn't just purely theoretical, but has an explicit relationship to the way we measure attitudes. Wilson, Lindsey and Schooler (2000) looked at the nature of what they call 'dual attitudes'. Most theoretical frameworks, which form the basis of the ways we measure attitudes and therefore feed back into more and more theories, work on the assumption that changes in attitudes lead to the *replacement* of an old attitude with a new one. Wilson et al. suggest that this is not necessarily true, but, rather, it is possible to hold dual attitudes. Sometimes, the explicit, measurable attitude can seem to have changed, but the old attitude, possibly something more extreme or less socially acceptable, remains below the surface, as an implicit attitude. It is even possible for attitudes that seem to contradict each other to co-exist, which can also mean we throw out data from some people because their responses on our questionnaires seem contradictory. At its heart, this is not as surprising as it might seem. We speak of the 'love–hate' relationship, without questioning that too much. It is possible to feel opposite things about something, even though logically it should not be. Somewhere, psychologists got carried away being scientific and forgot that human beings do not have to make sense. Not only are people sometimes illogical, but it actually doesn't matter. There is no rulebook on attitudes, but to some degree we have acted as if there were. People who seemed to believe two opposite things at once were considered irrational or mistaken, whereas it was the psychologists who had got it wrong by insisting that individuals must have some kind of internal logic to their emotions. Attitudes, we must also remember, have an emotional component, so it is hardly surprising that Wilson et al. should discover our attitudes are sometimes seemingly inconsistent.

Source: Wilson, T. D., Lindsey, S., & Schooler, T. Y. (2000). A model of dual attitudes. *Psychological Review, 107* 101–126.

Further reading Measuring attitudes

Topic	Key reading
This work outlines a particular method of measuring attitudes that involves getting respondents to indicate how their ratings compare with those of other people	Olson, J. M., Goffin, R. D., & Haynes, G. A. (2007). Relative versus absolute measures of explicit attitudes: Implications for predicting diverse attitude-relevant criteria. *Journal of Personality and Social Psychology, 93*, 907–926.
This meta-analysis shows how attitude studies can help us build theory on the relationship between attitudes and actual behaviour, a link not always as direct as one might imagine	Glasman, L. R., & Albarracín, D. (2006). Forming attitudes that predict future behavior: A meta-analysis of the attitude-behavior relation. *Psychological Bulletin, 132*, 778–822.

Chapter summary – pulling it all together

→ Can you tick all the points from the revision checklist at the beginning of this chapter?

→ Attempt the sample question from the beginning of this chapter using the answer guidelines below.

→ Go to the companion website at www.pearsoned.co.uk/psychologyexpress to access more revision support online, including interactive quizzes, flashcards, You be the marker exercises as well as answer guidance for the Test your knowledge and Sample questions from this chapter.

Answer guidelines

 Sample question   *Essay*

Discuss, with examples from the research literature, the notion that attitude measurement is as scientific as any other branch of psychology.

Approaching the question

Firstly, note that the question asks you to refer to the research literature, so you will have to think about what evidence you use and you will need to read a dozen or so relevant articles, as a minimum, to create the best possible answer. Note that you will also need to make a list of the relevant criteria for deciding that something is scientific.

Important points to include

- This question requires that you do some good research into the research that has been done using attitude surveys, so that you have some good (or bad, if you wish) examples of work that has been conducted.

- You also need to define 'science' operationally for this essay and everything you then say is to be put in the context of that. If you choose to take a view that science involves actual experiments, then attitude work isn't scientific, but mostly correlational in nature. Of course, a lot of psychology is like that. However, if you look at other definitions of science, which involve being systematic and controlled and proceeding in steps towards a better understanding, then attitude work could be seen to be scientific, albeit not experimental. Take your definitions of science and apply them to both the studies that you choose and psychology in general, point by point. Your essay will be finished easily this way.

Make your answer stand out

The quality of the examples of articles you find will mostly dictate whether your answer stands out for an essay like this. Choose carefully. A good answer will strike the right balance between the practical discussions of real-world research and the more theoretical, philosophical issues around what science really is.

Explore the accompanying website at www.pearsoned.co.uk/psychologyexpress

→ Prepare more effectively for exams and assignments using the answer guidelines for questions from this chapter.

→ Test your knowledge using multiple choice questions and flashcards.

→ Improve your essay skills by exploring the You be the marker exercises.

Notes

8

Reliability and validity

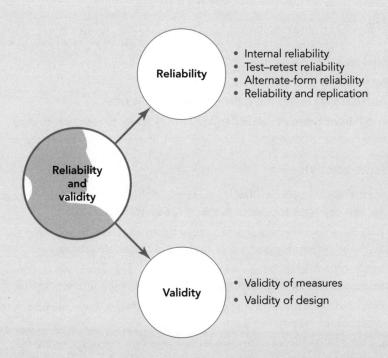

- Reliability
  - Internal reliability
  - Test–retest reliability
  - Alternate-form reliability
  - Reliability and replication

- Reliability and validity

- Validity
  - Validity of measures
  - Validity of design

A printable version of this topic map is available from
www.pearsoned.co.uk/psychologyexpress

Introduction

Reliability and validity are measures of the quality of research studies and their findings. It is, therefore, very important that you have a thorough knowledge and understanding of these crucial concepts and how they are applied to different types of research study in psychology. As with some of the other key concepts in research methods in psychology, it is relatively easy to learn the different types of reliability and validity as a list without really giving much thought to how they might actually be applied and used. While this is a necessary precursor to understanding, it is not sufficient in that you need to be able to demonstrate an in-depth understanding of the issues involved. While the information in this chapter is presented separately from the content of the other chapters, be aware that these issues cut across all types of research design, from experimental studies, through questionnaire measures, to observational studies.

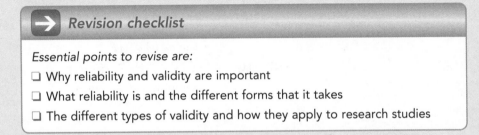

Revision checklist

Essential points to revise are:
- ❏ Why reliability and validity are important
- ❏ What reliability is and the different forms that it takes
- ❏ The different types of validity and how they apply to research studies

Assessment advice

- It is most likely that you will have encountered the issues of reliability and validity as a separate topic area within research methods.
- You may have been encouraged to apply these concepts to your own practical work when designing and carrying out your own studies.
- You might be asked to answer essay-style exam questions in which you define and discuss reliability and validity and how they are applied to research.
- You may also be presented with examples of studies to be evaluated in terms of reliability and validity.
- Make sure that you are able to make precise use of the appropriate terminology to refer to the different aspects of reliability and validity as they apply to the examples given.

Sample question

Could you answer this question? Opposite is a typical problem question that could arise on this topic.

Sample question **Problem-based learning**

Professor Totoro and Dr Catbus have each devised a scale intended to measure how much individuals love their partners. Each of their scales is made up of 30 items, each of which is measured on a 5-point Likert scale, where 1 = agree and 5 = disagree.

Professor Totoro has spent a great deal of time reading about the psychological theory concerning love and relationships, and has also conducted a series of informal interviews with a range of people in which he asked them what 'love' meant to them and the ways in which they thought about it, in terms of feelings, attitudes, thoughts and behaviour.

Dr Catbus put together a list of concepts related to 'love' as he considered it. He thought about the people, places and things that he loves and used his own thoughts and feelings to generate items.

The first six items from each of their scales are as follows.

Professor Totoro

1 I would do anything for my partner.

2 My partner is always there for me.

3 I find it easy to ignore my partner's faults.

4 I would find it hard to cope without my partner.

5 I feel miserable when I am separated from my partner.

6 I can tell my partner anything.

Dr Catbus

1 My partner and I both like chocolate.

2 I feel that my partner loves me.

3 My partner and I are both free to see other people if we want to.

4 When I am in love I find it difficult to concentrate.

5 I believe in love at first sight.

6 My partner thinks that the best kind of love grows out of a long friendship.

Bear in mind that Professor Totoro and Dr Catbus were both aiming to produce a measure of how much individuals love their partners.

1 Assess the face validity of both of the scales, as indicated by the example items listed above.

2 How could Professor Totoro and Dr Catbus establish the reliability of their scales? What problems may arise?

3 What issues may arise in the assessment of the validity of the scales?

Guidelines on answering this question are included at the end of this chapter, whilst further guidance on tackling other exam questions can be found on the companion website at: **www.pearsoned.co.uk/psychologyexpress**

Reliability

Reliability refers to the consistency and stability of a measure. This can be of two broad types: internal reliability, which refers to the extent to which individual elements are related, and external reliability, or consistency over time, which refers to how well the measure produces the same outcomes when used on different occasions or if presented in different forms.

Note that the use of the term 'reliable' is not quite the same as it is when used in everyday language. For example, if someone is always late for appointments, then we might complain of their being 'unreliable'. However, if the person is *always* late, without fail, then, in the sense in which the term is used by researchers, their behaviour is actually reliable, in that it is consistent and stable. A truly unreliable person is someone whose behaviour is unpredictable and inconsistent. The same applies to psychological measures; reliability is consistency.

Test your knowledge

8.1 What is meant by the reliability of a measure and how does this differ from the everyday use of the term?

An answer to this question can be found on the companion website at: www.pearsoned.co.uk/psychologyexpress

Internal reliability

Many measures in psychology are made up of several elements. This is especially true of questionnaire-type scales in which participants are asked to respond to a series of items. The responses to all of the items are combined to produce an overall 'score', which is intended to act as a measure of a particular concept (e.g. 'extroversion', 'depression', 'attitudes towards asylum seekers'). It is important that the individual items on a scale are all tapping into the same concept as each other, so if an individual responds in a certain way to one item, then they are likely to respond in a very similar way to the others. In other words, internal reliability refers to whether the individual elements of a measure are actually all measuring the same thing. The most common way of checking that this is the case is by calculating the 'split-half' reliability.

Split-half reliability

To calculate the split-half reliability, the items on the scale are divided into two sets, either by comparing the first half of the second with the second half or by taking alternate items (sometimes called 'odd–even reliability', as the odd-numbered and even-numbered items form two separate groups). The statistical details of this are beyond the scope of this book, but it involves the calculation of the correlation between the responses of individual participants to the two sets of items. If the measure is reliable, then there should be a high correlation between the two halves; a participant who scores 'high' on half of the items should also score 'high' on the other half and a participant who scores 'low' should do so on both halves of the measure.

While split-half reliability can give a good indication of the internal reliability of a measure, it can be difficult to determine where the problem lies should the two halves of the scale not correlate particularly well. A more sophisticated approach is to calculate Cronbach's alpha. This works by splitting the items into all of the possible halves and then calculating the average of all of the possible split-half reliabilities. Because all of the combinations of items are used, if a particular item is causing a problem, it can easily be identified and removed from the scale.

Further reading Internal reliability	
Topic	Key reading
A general discussion of the application of Cronbach's alpha to psychological measures	Ponterotto, J., & Ruckdeschel, D. (2007). An overview of coefficient alpha and a reliability matrix for estimating adequacy of internal consistency coefficients with psychological research measures. *Perceptual & Motor Skills, 105*(3), 997–1014.
An example of how internal reliability is applied to an intelligence test	Ryan, J., Glass, L., & Bartels, J. (2009). Internal consistency reliability of the WISC-IV among primary school students. *Psychological Reports, 104*(3), 874–878.
Reliability of a happiness scale (this is also relevant to construct validity, see later)	Robbins, M., Francis, L., & Edwards, B. (2010). Happiness as stable extraversion: Internal consistency reliability and construct validity of the Oxford Happiness Questionnaire among undergraduate students. *Current Psychology, 29*(2), 89–94.

Internal reliability versus external reliability

There is a trade-off between internal reliability and the reliability of the measure when used on different occasions. In order to increase the internal reliability of a measure, the 'bad' items can be removed. This will result in a measure that has fewer items. Shorter scales tend to have lower reliability over time, so it is important to strike a balance between increasing the internal reliability of a measure while retaining enough items to ensure consistency over time.

To fully understand why this is the case it is, of course, important to know how external reliability, or consistency over time, is measured, what can influence it and why it is important.

Test your knowledge

8.2 How is Cronbach's alpha related to split-half reliability?

8.3 Why is there a trade-off between internal reliability and reliability over time?

Answers to these questions can be found on the companion website at: **www.pearsoned.co.uk/psychologyexpress**

Test–retest reliability

A test that is reliable should produce the same results on different occasions, so if the same participants are tested on two separate occasions, there should be a high correlation between the two scores produced. It is, however, very important to appreciate this applies only to tests that measure psychological concepts that are thought to be stable over time. For example, if a measure of mood is used, participants might be in a good mood one day, but feel totally miserable the next or vice versa. Their score on the test will, as a result, be completely different on the two occasions. The test–retest reliability measure will be very low, but this does not, in this example, mean that the measure itself is not a reliable measure of mood. In contrast, a diagnostic test for dyslexia in a group of schoolchildren should produce very similar outcomes for individuals on separate occasions, as dyslexia is not something that comes and goes. If this test results in different subsets of children being diagnosed as having dyslexia each time the test is used, then its test–retest reliability will be low.

Further reading Test–retest reliability	
Topic	Key reading
An example of how a test is developed and its test–retest reliability determined; validity is also discussed	Fontenelle, I., Prazeres, A., Borges, M., Rangé, B., Versiani, M., & Fontenelle, L. (2010). The Brazilian Portuguese version of the saving inventory – revised: Internal consistency, test–retest reliability, and validity of a questionnaire to assess hoarding. *Psychological Reports, 106*(1), 279–296.
Application of test–retest reliability to a specific task (rather than a questionnaire-based measure)	Goertz, C., Kolling, T., Frahsek, S., Stanisch, A., & Knopf, M. (2008). Assessing declarative memory in 12-month-old infants: A test–retest reliability study of the deferred imitation task. *European Journal of Developmental Psychology, 5*(4), 492–506.

Other factors influencing test–retest reliability

By definition, the calculation of test–retest reliability involves administering the same test twice to the same participants and comparing the individual results. In addition to the possibility that the measure is intended to tap into a concept that is not expected to be stable over time, there are other factors that can impact upon the calculated test–retest reliability and it is important to be aware of these.

The 'score' that someone gets on the same test on the second occasion can, of course, be affected by the fact that it is their second time. Participants may simply remember how they responded the first time and deliberately say the same again so as to appear consistent, even if they feel slightly different this time. As a result of this, the calculation of test–retest reliability can make a measure appear to be much more reliable than it actually is.

In a more general way, familiarity with the test being used and the type of questions being asked can make participants feel more relaxed on the second occasion than they were the first time around. It is important to bear in mind that test–retest reliability, and the concepts of reliability more generally, apply to the whole range of quantifiable measures used by psychologists, not just to self-rating scales. Intelligence tests, for example, require people to solve puzzles and undertake reasoning tasks. People who are more familiar with the types of question that these tests feature tend to perform generally better. This may produce artificially higher scores on the second attempt at the test.

Test your knowledge

8.4 What is test–retest reliability? What factors can influence it? If familiarity with the test produces better performance on the second occasion, how, exactly, would this affect test–retest reliability? (Think carefully about this!)

An answer to this question can be found on the companion website at: **www.pearsoned.co.uk/psychologyexpress**

Further reading Test–retest reliability and practice effects

Topic	Key reading
An example of how practice effects can be dealt with when considering test–retest reliability	Bird, C., Papadopoulou, K., Ricciardelli, P., Rossor, M., & Cipolotti, L. (2003). Test–retest reliability, practice effects and reliable change indices for the recognition memory test. *British Journal of Clinical Psychology, 42*(4), 407–425.

Alternate-form reliability

In a way, alternate-form reliability (also known as 'parallel forms') combines the concepts of split-half reliability and test–retest reliability. An 'alternate form' of a test is, basically, a different set of questions from those employed in the original version. This means that, with stable concepts, participants should score roughly the same on both versions. This overcomes the problems associated with participants simply remembering and reproducing their answers on the second test and can, therefore, allow a more accurate calculation of the reliability of the measures.

Further reading Alternate-form reliability

Topic	Key reading
An example of the use of alternate-form reliability	Wyatt, B., Conners, F., & Carr, M. (1998). The Snodgrass picture fragment completion test: Alternate-form reliability. *Behavior Research Methods, Instruments, & Computers, 30*(2), 360.

Reliability and replication

The reliability of measures is closely associated with the replicability of effects. Simply put, if the measures are not reliable, then any studies that make use of those measures will not be reliable either. If the results of those studies are not reliable, then it will not be possible to replicate the study and find the same effects as those reported. In this very direct way, reliability and replication are closely related as both refer to stability: reliability to the stability of a measure over time; and replication to the stability of effects.

Test your knowledge

8.5 What are the problems associated with measuring test–retest reliability?

8.6 What is meant by 'alternate-form reliability' and how far can this address the problems associated with test–retest reliability?

8.7 What is the link between reliability and replicability?

Answers to these questions can be found on the companion website at: **www.pearsoned.co.uk/psychologyexpress**

Validity

Where reliability refers to the internal consistency of a measure or to its stability over time or in alternative forms, validity is to do with whether the measure is actually measuring what it's supposed to be measuring. An understanding of the distinction between validity and reliability is very important. A measure could be reliable, but that does not necessarily mean it is valid. For example, a properly calibrated set of bathroom scales will produce pretty much the same score for any individual from one day to the next. This is, therefore, a reliable measure and a valid way of measuring weight. If, however, the 'score' obtained from the bathroom scales were used as a measure of mood, then this would not be valid. A measure can, therefore, be reliable without being valid.

As previously mentioned, where a concept is being measured that is not expected to be stable, the notion of test–retest reliability becomes less important (e.g. people's moods can vary widely from one day to the next). Validity remains important, in that a test designed to measure mood must be doing just that, even if it does not have demonstrable test–retest reliability.

Validity can, as shown above, refer to the *measure* being used, but can also be discussed in terms of a research study in its entirety, including the broader aspects of *design* and how these impact upon the generalisability of the study's findings.

There are several different subtypes of validity, as shown in Figure 8.1. These aspects of validity are defined in the sections below.

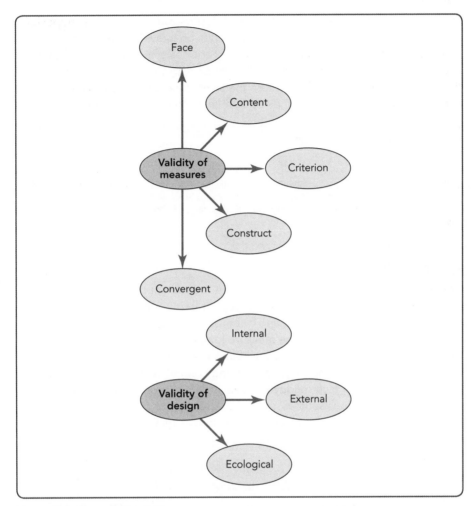

Figure 8.1 **Aspects of validity**

Validity of measures

Face validity

Does the content of the test *look* as though it is measuring what it is supposed to? Face validity is very subjective and depends on individual judgement. Questions that are clearly related to the concept being measured are reassuring and less confusing for participants and it can be risky to make an assumption that less direct items will also measure the same concept, at least without careful analysis of how the measure stands up in relation to other types of validity.

Further reading Face validity	
Topic	*Key reading*
Demonstrates how face validity can be manipulated (and so helps to illustrate what face validity is)	Yuching Ni, S., & Hauenstein, N. (1998). Applicant reactions to personality tests: Effects of item invasiveness and face validity. *Journal of Business & Psychology, 12*(4), 391–406.

Content validity

Content validity is similar to face validity, but is more sophisticated and involved. In order to measure a psychological concept, it is important to cover the full range of aspects of that concept and not miss anything out. So, while face validity is a check on whether the measure looks like it is measuring the right thing, content validity can be thought of as more of a check on whether it is measuring the right thing *fully*. Establishing content validity is much more involved than judging face validity because it depends on the gathering of information from various sources, such as published research, other researchers in the field or from using pilot studies to explore aspects of the to-be-measured concept that are of relevance to potential participants.

Test your knowledge

8.11 What is face validity and how does this differ from content validity?

An answer to this question can be found on the companion website at: **www.pearsoned.co.uk/psychologyexpress**

Criterion validity

If a test is supposed to measure a particular concept, then it should correlate with other established measures of the same thing, taken at the same time from the same individuals. For example, if we want to check that a new, short questionnaire has criterion validity, we can try it out by using it alongside a well-established, longer questionnaire we would like to replace. If the new, short measure is measuring the same concept as the longer old one, then participants will respond similarly to both and the scores will be correlated for the sample. The validity of the measure is thus gauged by how well it measures up to a particular criterion, hence the name.

Convergent validity

Convergent validity is similar to the idea of criterion validity, but it also emphasises the importance of comparing different *types* of measures, which should also correlate if they are measuring the same concept. For instance, a self-rated questionnaire of aggression should correlate not only with other questionnaire measures of the same thing, but should also be related to behavioural measures, such as an aggressive response to a frustrating task in an experiment. The restriction of judgements about validity to the comparison of measures of the same type can be problematic because it may be, for example, while two questionnaires about a particular issue seem to be measuring the same concept, neither might be related to an individual's behaviour as measured by other direct means that may have even greater face and content validity.

Test your knowledge

8.12 What is meant by criterion validity and convergent validity and how are they different?

An answer to this question can be found on the companion website at: www.pearsoned.co.uk/psychologyexpress

Further reading Criterion and convergent validity

Topic	Key reading
An example of how criterion validity can be assessed	Kills Small, N., Simons, J., & Stricherz, M. (2007). Assessing criterion validity of the Simple Screening Instrument for Alcohol and Other Drug Abuse (SSI-AOD) in a college population. *Addictive Behaviors, 32*(10), 2425–2431.
Another example, focusing on cognitive tests	Luo, D., Thompson, L., & Detterman, D. (2006). The criterion validity of tasks of basic cognitive processes. *Intelligence, 34*(1), 79–120
An example of the application of convergent validity	Breitenbecher, K. (2008). The convergent validities of two measures of dating behaviors related to risk for sexual victimization. *Journal of Interpersonal Violence, 23*(8), 1095–1107.

Construct validity

Construct validity is, arguably, the aspect of the validity of a measure that is most directly relevant to the question of whether it is actually measuring the underlying psychological concept or construct in question. While other aspects of validity focus on whether the test seems to be measuring the same thing as other, more established, tests, there is always the possibility that none of them is actually truly valid. In essence, the examination of construct validity involves going back to first principles and exploring, in depth, the theoretical ideas that underpin the concept being measured. For example, a questionnaire measure of 'happiness' could be put together fairly quickly and it would be fairly straightforward to ensure that it had high face validity. It would only have high construct validity if the whole psychological concept of happiness, how it is constructed and how psychologists have developed ideas and theories about happiness were examined very carefully. This relates very closely to the ideas about the development of theory and ways of testing theories summarised in the first two chapters of this book. This is an important consideration because it ensures that measures are based very squarely on a conceptual understanding rather than just on comparison with other, presumably valid, measures.

Test your knowledge

8.13 What is construct validity and why is it, arguably, the most important form of validity?

An answer to this question can be found on the companion website at: www.pearsoned.co.uk/psychologyexpress

---

Further reading Construct validity

Topic	Key reading
An exploration of the construct validity of a personality trait	Lounsbury, J., Levy, J., Park, S., Gibson, L., & Smith, R. (2009). An investigation of the construct validity of the personality trait of self-directed learning. *Learning & Individual Differences, 19*(4), 411–418.
Another example of how construct validity is discussed and explored	Japuntich, S., Piper, M., Schlam, T., Bolt, D., & Baker, T. (2009). Do smokers know what we're talking about? The construct validity of nicotine dependence questionnaire measures. *Psychological Assessment, 21*(4), 595–607.

Validity of design

The other aspect of validity that can be considered is the validity of the study as a whole and of its design. This is especially applicable to experimental studies.

Internal validity of experiments

All of the efforts that experimenters make to control experiments are designed to maintain the internal validity of an experiment. An experiment is designed with one purpose in mind: to establish whether the manipulation of the independent variable has an effect on the dependent variables in order to test an hypothesis about the link between the two. An experiment that achieves this goal has high internal validity, because, basically, it has done what it set out to do. If you relate this back to your understanding and knowledge of experimental design, you will see that there are several ways in which experiments can fail to achieve high internal validity. All of the issues of control such as imbalanced groups, demand characteristics, experiment effects, confounding variables and so on are threats to internal validity. If, for example, the differences between two groups are not due to the manipulation of the independent variable, but are due to a confounding variable, then the experiment will have low internal validity.

Test your knowledge

8.14 Explain how the control of an experiment is concerned with its internal validity and give examples of the threats to internal validity.

An answer to this question can be found on the companion website at: **www.pearsoned.co.uk/psychologyexpress**

External validity and generalisability

A carefully controlled experiment will have high internal validity and it may be found that the manipulation of the independent variable had a significant effect on the dependent variable. It does not, however, follow that the results will be generalisable to other samples, contexts, sets of stimuli and so on. The issues surrounding generalisability are really a matter of the external validity of a study. This is an easy distinction to remember. Internal validity is to do with the control of the experiment as a self-contained enterprise and external validity refers to the application of the results of that experiment externally.

There is a balance to be struck between ensuring internal validity and external validity. On the one hand, an experiment that is very narrowly constrained in terms of the sample, the materials used and the procedure will be internally valid, but the results may be limited in their generalisability. On the other hand, an experiment that is designed to offer greater generalisability of its findings may have a looser design, be less well controlled and so have lower internal validity.

Test your knowledge

8.15 Explain the relationship between external validity and the generalisability of a study's findings.

An answer to this question can be found on the companion website at: **www.pearsoned.co.uk/psychologyexpress**

CRITICAL FOCUS

Ecological validity

The term 'ecological validity' is often used in criticism of laboratory-based experiments for lacking 'realism' and for not being as generalisable as studies conducted out in the 'real world'. Many psychology undergraduate students often automatically criticise laboratory experiments as having low ecological validity and, therefore, as having less value than more naturalistic studies. This is a very narrow and superficial view and demonstrates a lack of understanding of the concepts of validity and generalisability. In this sense, arguing that a study has low ecological validity is merely to say that it is 'unrealistic'. This is a subjective opinion that has no objective definition. Also, while the *study* and the tasks that participants undertake might be artificial and contrived for the purposes of the laboratory study, they can still reveal important things about the ways in which people think, perceive and behave. The task is to then attempt to replicate the findings and to explore their application to the 'real world'.

Be very careful about assuming that 'naturalistic' studies have greater validity and generalisability. While they may take place in 'real' situations and settings, the quality of the data collected may be contaminated by any number of extraneous factors. 'Ecological validity' is most fruitfully thought of as a version of 'external validity'. To argue that 'real-world' studies are necessarily better due to higher 'ecological validity' does not provide any kind of explanation or theoretical account that can be brought to bear on the research process.

Further reading Ecological validity

Topic	Key reading
The ecological validity of mock juror paradigms	Breau, D., & Brook, B. (2007). 'Mock' mock juries: A field experiment on the ecological validity of jury simulations. *Law & Psychology Review, 31*, 77–92.
An interesting consideration of the assessment of credibility in police interviews	Gozna, L. (2007). Tackling ecological validity: Conducting observations in a police-suspect interview. *Issues in Forensic Psychology, 6*, 57–63.

Chapter summary – pulling it all together

→ Can you tick all the points from the revision checklist at the beginning of this chapter?

→ Attempt the sample question from the beginning of this chapter using the answer guidelines opposite.

→ Go to the companion website at www.pearsoned.co.uk/psychologyexpress to access more revision support online, including interactive quizzes, flashcards, You be the marker exercises as well as answer guidance for the Test your knowledge and Sample questions from this chapter.

Further reading for Chapter 8

Topic	Key reading
Validity and reliability of qualitative studies	Madill, A., Jordan, A., & Shirley, C. (2000). Objectivity and reliability in qualitative analysis: Realist, contextualist and radical. *British Journal of Psychology, 91*(1), 1–20.
	Moret, M., Reuzel, R., Van der Wilt, G., & Grin, J. (2007). Validity and reliability of qualitative data analysis: Interobserver agreement in reconstructing interpretative frames. *Field Methods, 19*(1), 24–39.
	Pyett, P. (2003). Validation of qualitative research in the 'real world'. *Qualitative Health Research, 13*(8), 1170–1179.

Answer guidelines

 Sample question   *Problem-based learning*

Professor Totoro and Dr Catbus have each devised a scale intended to measure how much individuals love their partners. Each of their scales is made up of 30 items, each of which is measured on a 5-point Likert scale, where 1 = agree and 5 = disagree.

Professor Totoro has spent a great deal of time reading about the psychological theory concerning love and relationships and has also conducted a series of informal interviews with a range of people in which he asked them what 'love' meant to them and the ways in which they thought about it, in terms of feelings, attitudes, thoughts and behaviour.

Dr Catbus put together a list of concepts related to 'love' as he considered it. He thought about the people, places and things that he loves and used his own thoughts and feelings to generate items.

The first six items from each of their scales are as follows.

Professor Totoro

1 I would do anything for my partner.

2 My partner is always there for me.

3 I find it easy to ignore my partner's faults.

4 I would find it hard to cope without my partner.

5 I feel miserable when I am separated from my partner.

6 I can tell my partner anything.

Dr Catbus

1 My partner and I both like chocolate.

2 I feel that my partner loves me.

3 My partner and I are both free to see other people if we want to.

4 When I am in love I find it difficult to concentrate.

5 I believe in love at first sight.

6 My partner thinks that the best kind of love grows out of a long friendship.

131

Bear in mind that Professor Totoro and Dr Catbus were both aiming to produce a measure of how much individuals love their partners.

1 Assess the face validity of both of the scales, as indicated by the example items listed above.

2 How could Professor Totoro and Dr Catbus establish the reliability of their scales? What problems may arise?

3 What issues may arise in the assessment of the validity of the scales?

Approaching the question

The question requires you to apply the concepts of reliability and validity to the development of two scales. In approaching the question, the key point to remember is that you must show you are *applying* the concepts and not merely reciting them. While, for example, demonstrating that you know a definition of 'reliability' is essential, you must make a specific effort to show how this applies to the analysis of the two scales under development. In particular, pay attention to the content of the scales and the underlying concept that they are intended to measure. If you address the issues in general terms, you will not be able to show that you have a thorough understanding of how to apply the concepts in specific cases.

Important points to include

● The question requires an understanding and discussion of reliability and validity, so there is going to be quite a lot of ground to cover. Throughout your answer, it will be crucial to demonstrate your understanding of the full range of concepts and how they apply to the particular example.

● With questions like this one, you must pay careful attention to all of the information provided and think about how it can help you to answer the question. For example, do not overlook the processes that the two researchers undertook in order to develop the items for their respective scales. This information has not been provided by accident. If you have the appropriate conceptual understanding, you will be able to relate these processes to at least two aspects of validity and discuss how and why one of the two scales may be likely to have higher validity than the other.

● Make sure you work your way through systematically so that you cover all of the different aspects of reliability and validity. Think about what is being measured. Is it likely to be a stable concept or not and how would this impact on the measurement of test–retest reliability?

● In terms of criterion validity and convergent validity, think about how the underlying construct might be measured in different ways. What other measures could be used to see whether the scales are valid?

- Last, and by no means least, make sure that you do not get reliability and validity mixed up! If you really understand the different aspects of each, you should not have any difficulty with this as you discuss them and apply them to the question in hand.

Make your answer stand out

Your answer will stand out if you show that you have read around some of the issues and have a deeper understanding than just being able to supply accurate definitions and examples. The introduction of ecological validity to your answer, along with an understanding that it encapsulates much more than 'realism' would demonstrate a sophisticated level of understanding. Generally, take the opportunity to introduce discussion of replicability and generalisability and how they relate to reliability and validity. Take Professor Totoro and Dr Catbus further down the road and consider how they might be able to use their scales (if reliable and valid) and how they would be generalisable to different times, contexts and participant samples.

If you really want to go the extra mile, and immerse yourself in a fuller consideration of reliability and validity, you might consider how these issues can be applied to qualitative research studies, as discussed by the articles in the last Further reading section.

Explore the accompanying website at www.pearsoned.co.uk/psychologyexpress

→ Prepare more effectively for exams and assignments using the answer guidelines for questions from this chapter.
→ Test your knowledge using multiple choice questions and flashcards.
→ Improve your essay skills by exploring the You be the marker exercises.

Notes

Notes

9

Qualitative approaches and methods

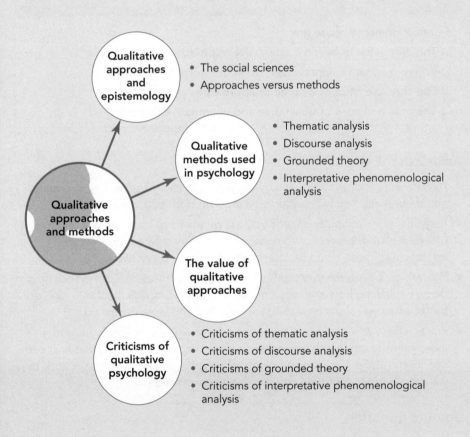

- Qualitative approaches and epistemology
  - The social sciences
  - Approaches versus methods

- Qualitative methods used in psychology
  - Thematic analysis
  - Discourse analysis
  - Grounded theory
  - Interpretative phenomenological analysis

- Qualitative approaches and methods

- The value of qualitative approaches

- Criticisms of qualitative psychology
  - Criticisms of thematic analysis
  - Criticisms of discourse analysis
  - Criticisms of grounded theory
  - Criticisms of interpretative phenomenological analysis

A printable version of this topic map is available from
www.pearsoned.co.uk/psychologyexpress

Introduction

Qualitative approaches to research are still quite new to psychology, but they are developing rapidly. Unfortunately, they are often misunderstood, with many students thinking that they are an 'easy option' in order to avoid statistics. The first thing you should be aware of is that this is really not the case. Qualitative approaches are very varied and can involve a lot of hard work. In fact, often a qualitative piece of research involves more work than a quantitative one. You will need to know about a range of approaches and why a qualitative approach and a qualitative method are *related* but different things.

→ *Revision checklist*

Essential points to revise are:
- ❏ The difference between a qualitative approach and a method
- ❏ Where qualitative approaches 'sit' in the world of research
- ❏ The characteristics of a range of approaches and methods
- ❏ The pros and cons of qualitative and quantitative research

Assessment advice

- Assessments concerning qualitative psychology can take two forms: practical and theoretical. You will probably have to do both as a student.
- In typical examination questions you will be asked to state the key features of a particular approach or compare and contrast different qualitative approaches. These could be in essay form or as short answers.
- You will do best when you don't simply list the features, but can elaborate on them, explaining how and why they are important. As a general rule, you do better when you show how things fit together and work in context.
- Practical assessments in qualitative research usually come in the form of an assignment to conduct some research itself or to analyse a text that is already provided. Always give yourself plenty of time for these activities, because they will stretch out longer than you had initially expected.

Sample question

Could you answer this question? Opposite is a typical essay question that could arise on this topic.

Sample question   *Essay*

What is the value of qualitative research? Illustrate your answer with reference to two approaches.

Guidelines on answering this question are included at the end of this chapter, whilst further guidance on tackling other exam questions can be found on the companion website at: **www.pearsoned.co.uk/psychologyexpress**

Qualitative approaches and epistemology

Firstly, it is important to know what 'epistemology' means. It is the theory of knowledge or, in other words, it is the name given to our study of our study of the world! It is a branch of philosophy devoted to the issues around finding things out and what it means to know something, to research something, and it is a discourse on the difficult issue of whether 'facts' really exist. It is related to *ontology*, which is the study of what it means to exist. It represents a fundamental academic approach to knowledge and, at the same time, it is a step back from the day-to-day work of the researcher. The average researcher works to find things out, but does not necessarily trouble themselves about the point of it all. In epistemology, we look precisely at that issue. We debate the point of knowledge, the point of study, the point of research and so on. It is a way of keeping our expansion of knowledge in check and preventing us from becoming a little too arrogant about our so-called progress. In fact, in epistemological terms, the notion of progress must also be examined.

Historically, the philosophers of epistemology had very little to do with the scientific researchers. They worked separately, in different laboratories and offices, without any cross-fertilisation of ideas. Mostly, they did not talk to each other, carrying out their independent work and often not seeing the value in each others' labours. The average research scientist conducting experiments, including psychologists using quantitative methods, did not question their work at the most fundamental level. They took for granted the notion that there was such a thing as meaning, as progress, as fact. One could easily argue that if they were to start to address these issues they would be distracted from their work. However, this was something that a chemist could argue much more easily than a psychologist could. A chemist might mix substances together and watch what happens to them in a beaker, in a laboratory, at a particular temperature and pressure. The wider world and the meaning of knowledge is not so important, in that two substances almost always do exactly the same thing in the same conditions. There is no social context, as it were. Naturally, this doesn't apply to psychology. We study behaviour, but of complex organisms like human animals, and that cannot be understood outside of a wider context and environment. Human beings are social, political, dynamic, volitional, sarcastic and contrary at times. Chemicals never are.

In the 1960s, societies in the Western world were changing and people had begun to question everything. It was fashionable to do so. Along with hippie culture came new ways of challenging things, including a rise in qualitative methods of enquiry. Psychology embraced this and became a new form of science, much less obsessed with following the strict scientific methods that had dominated us for a century or so. The hard-line scientific methods were certainly not abandoned (they flourish today), but we started to open the door to new ways of understanding the world. Those new ways were qualitative approaches and methods and they were on the front line in the development of the so-called 'social sciences'.

The social sciences

Qualitative methods developed into fully fledged research tools, it will be no surprise to you to learn, from the social sciences. In turn, they took the idea from the philosophers. There is more to knowledge than experimental methods, with strict controls, randomisation, sampling frames and so on. Researchers started to realise that if you want to know some things about people, sometimes you have to *ask* them. To be fair, we had always known this, but we had usually tried to keep asking people things *away* from science, because we believed that interviews and self-reports were unreliable, invalid and generally raised

CRITICAL FOCUS

The social sciences

You might have realised something interesting about the history of the development of both qualitative methods and the social sciences. Essentially, it is the old question of the chicken and the egg. Which came first? Did society start changing, which led to academia changing, causing the social sciences to form? Or did academia start to change, giving rise to the social sciences, making society alter? The thing to remember is that, although historians generate theories about this, it is almost impossible to know what happened. In the twentieth century, many things changed. All of those things were part of society, including researchers and academics, but, equally, researchers and academics helped shape the world around them. As psychologists, we might study teenage pregnancy *because it happens*. We didn't make it happen, though. However, social networking websites have become a widespread phenomenon *because someone invented them*. The traffic is two-way and developments are very hard to spot at a particular point in time or place. When there is a tail-back on the motorway, which particular driver 'caused' it? Someone must have, mustn't they? What history teaches us is that simple cause and effect is not the way of human development. It's another reason why qualitative research has become stronger over time; it is much less concerned with the oversimplifications of cause and effect.

more questions than they answered. Now, here is the important bit: qualitative researchers argued that traditional science is also fundamentally flawed and not necessarily any more reliable or valid. Furthermore, they said that, if some things can be discovered only by interviewing people, there is no reason to leave that line of enquiry untouched. Just because something is difficult doesn't mean we should not try to do it.

Approaches versus methods

An approach is much more philosophical than a method, although they are tied up together. Proponents of a particular approach tend to use a particular method and they often have the same name, which is why students can easily become confused. Grounded theory, for example, is the name of a specific way of viewing reality and the place of research in that reality. However, commonly people say 'grounded theory' when they mean the method of analysis of data that grounded theorists use. In one way or another, many qualitative researchers are social constructionists (believing that everything is constructed by the people who use it, including behaviour and society) and many of them are critical psychologists (believing that we should question all our values and assumptions as a matter of course). However, you should be aware of a growing number of psychologists who are neither social constructionists, nor critical psychologists and are very much like the old-fashioned scientists, but they use qualitative methods in their research. They believe that you *can* find things out and there are *facts* in the world to be discovered and there is *value* in *progress*. They use qualitative methods, but their approach isn't really a qualitative one. Can you see the difference? To them, qualitative methods are a tool and that's all. This causes quite a lot of debate in modern psychology, sometimes very animated.

Test your knowledge

9.1 What is epistemology and why is it important to understanding qualitative approaches to research?

An answer to this question can be found on the companion website at:
www.pearsoned.co.uk/psychologyexpress

Qualitative methods used in psychology

So, we can now focus on the key qualitative methods and approaches that are used in psychology. Many of the methods described here come in various forms, so there isn't just one way to do each of them. Whilst that is difficult for a student trying to learn about them, it is crucial to qualitative research itself that there is flexibility and variety inherent in it. What makes it special makes it frustrating, in equal measure. Therefore, when you read about qualitative research, be aware that there are dozens of forms of discourse analysis, for example. Some people even use hybrid techniques, drawing together elements of more than one approach or method.

Thematic analysis

This is one of the oldest (and some would say most basic) forms of qualitative analysis and is very popular outside of psychology, in nursing and healthcare research, for example. It involves *coding* texts, reading and rereading them and noticing various words or concepts that seem to be recurring. These become codes, then on further reading these codes can be adapted and modified, by either joining some together under a new conceptual umbrella or splitting them into two. Essentially, you have to keep doing this until you believe you have gone as far as you can. This idea of continuing with analysis until you cannot go any further is a key one in qualitative research and is known as *saturation*.

The main steps for a thematic analysis could be described thus.

1 Firstly, read the data items in order to become very familiar with them.
2 After a number of readings, start taking note of patterns that emerge.
3 Make note of the patterns in relation to the context in which they occur.
4 Find quotations where these things are illustrated.
5 Think carefully about the patterns, trying to understand what is being implied or suggested by the interview respondents or writers of the texts. Group these together.
6 These groups become your themes, then you can begin to consider how those themes might interlock, interact or split into smaller subthemes.

Obviously, as you can see, there is an element of interpretation involved in thematic analysis. This is something that some qualitative researchers find unacceptable, which is one reason why other methods have become more popular, including discourse analysis.

Discourse analysis

Discourse analysis is a blanket term describing no fewer than eight main types of approach and analysis. Some would say that there are dozens of published types of discourse analysis. Each one is different in a number of ways and, for example, Parker (1992) states that there are around 20 steps to conducting a Foucauldian discourse analysis, although, like many authors, Parker resists suggesting that this is the only way to conduct the analysis. Therefore, the key thing to remember is that there are many types of discourse analysis, each one is different and each one has its own characteristics, but there should not be prescriptions about how to do discourse analysis. Each researcher can, to some extent, 'do their own thing' although this does not mean that 'anything goes'.

One of the important elements of discourse analysis is the frequent use of conversation analysis and the Jefferson transcription system. This allows the researcher to use a kind of shorthand to codify transcripts easily and break language used down into units of discourse. Most conversation (but not necessarily all) is best characterised by *turn-taking*. Furthermore, discourse analysis places ultimate value on the *text*. A text can be anything, such as a conversation, a book, a newspaper article, a mime act or a television programme. Discourse analysts assert that this is all there is. Beyond the text, there is nothing and all meaning comes from the text and the reading of the text. They are not interested in discovering something 'behind' a text, because the text is all there is.

Potter and Wetherell (1987) describe eight main steps (that unfold into ten) for the conduct of discourse analysis:

1 Firstly, you decide upon your research question. Often, this occurs a long time before you even begin to think about analysis or data. A research question can be something you wish to know more about that goes back decades or it might relate entirely to a new phenomenon that has very little history.

2 Next, you decide on where to get your data from, i.e. your sample. Obviously, you get the right data from asking the right people.

3 Collecting records. Your own recollection of events is very flawed and, although qualitative analysis allows for the fact that all knowledge is socially constructed, it would be rather pointless to start off with poor records. You need to collect all pertinent information that applies to a particular text you wish to analyse.

4 Interviewing. You conduct your interviews, as much as possible involving naturally occurring talk rather than set questions. Open interviews should be as open as possible whilst remaining loyal to the research question.

5 Transcribing. This might involve using a specific transcription method bringing out the nuances of the conversation or could be more like the script of a play.

6 Coding. Work through the data noting codes that you feel are in some way indicative of the flow of the conversation or text or, indeed, where you believe the conversation might be broken up. Look for words or ideas that seem like pins holding the talk together. Codes can be big ideas or small ones.

7 Analysis. This can be done in many ways, but involves deconstructing the text to look for the ways in which it is created and the exchange of turns that form the text should be noted, along with your own reactions to them and your reasons for reading the text the way you have. This is likely to keep changing as you read on.

8 You go through again, looking for things you didn't see before, noting how your reading of the text varies and changes and how your ideas develop. Keep a careful record of *repertoires* used and their contexts.

9 Validation. In this stage you would tie together the different elements of your analysis. Look for coherence, note the relationship between the speakers and the speech and make clear what you believe is unexplained or what is striking about your reading of the data.

10 Writing up. This is where you express your reading of the text to others. Bear in mind that this is all it is. You are presenting your version of events.

Key term

An **interpretative repertoire** is a particular set of words or phrases or ways of expression, such as tones of voice, which is used in a particular context by a particular person. You might notice in a transcript that whenever someone refers to their own behaviour or ideas they say 'kind of' or 'sort of', but when they refer to someone else they say 'do you know what I mean?' This might be worth noting and, certainly, could be characterised as part of a repertoire. 'Kind of' and 'sort of' are phrases that one might read as an expression of doubt or vagueness, whereas 'do you know what I mean?' could express a questioning of the other speaker. In one case, the person questions themselves, in another case they question the interviewer, for example.

Grounded theory

Grounded theory (Glaser & Strauss, 1967) is based upon a fundamental principle that theory should emerge from data, rather than data being collected around a particular theory, to support or refute it. Normally, in science, we test theories by experimenting. This, some say, means that we only find the things we expect to find. Whilst this is not quite true, since much research in the sciences churns up unexpected findings that make us change our ideas entirely, it is the case that we often can spend a lot of time and energy pursuing things based on what we presuppose the world is like. What would happen if we didn't start with theories, but simply a research question, then let the data do the talking? This is the founding principle of grounded theory.

Grounded theory is, in many ways, an extension of thematic analysis, in that both rely on coding and similar approaches to discovering themes, but the addition of the philosophy of grounded theory (themes emerge and are not theory-driven) helps set it apart from thematic analysis.

To conduct a grounded theory analysis you need to start off as a grounded theory researcher. This isn't a method of analysis you can simply tag on to a different approach. It certainly requires subscribing to a particular philosophy and ontology.

Interviews are often held by simply allowing a person to talk on a subject, with little or no preparation or set questions. Once the interviews are transcribed, one begins with a process of open coding, finding the initial ideas that emerge from the data. Then, axial coding ensues, where codes are joined together where they relate to each other. Throughout the process, one makes comparisons between codes using what is called the *method of constant comparison*. As examples of codes occur in different contexts, you must explore the variety of uses of those codes, looking for differences and similarities that pull them apart and bind them together. As things occur to you, you keep a paper trail so you can follow your own thinking later, including taking theoretical memos so, as the theories emerge from the data, you can track their progress and keep an eye on the thoughts that led you there. This allows other researchers to keep track of your theory development and to question it themselves.

As you progress, you might feel the need to go back to your participants or interviewees, asking them to elaborate on things that have emerged from what they said previously, collecting more data in the light of the theories which you are building from the existing data. You would do this, theoretically, over and over again until you feel that you've said everything you can say on a subject. This does not mean that the subject is truly exhausted, but merely that you have reached a stopping point of your own. Someone else could take over at this point, working in the same area, refining or rejecting your theories.

KEY STUDY

Putting off until tomorrow what you can do today...

Schraw, Wadkins and Olafson (2007) present a grounded theory study of something that should be relevant and interesting to lecturers and students alike: academic procrastination. This is defined as putting things off instead of doing them, but some have argued it should have three characteristics, i.e. it must be unnecessary, counterproductive and dilatory (which means that it should involve wasting time). Schraw et al. define procrastination more simply, as 'intentionally deferring or delaying work that must be completed' (p. 13).

The authors conducted interviews with 67 students, which might seem a large number for a qualitative study, but in fact not all qualitative research is necessarily small-scale. Grounded theory work often involves multi-stage interviews with large numbers.

They found that, after various levels of coding and analysis, a model emerged containing six principles. These were *minimum time, optimum efficiency, peak affective experience, early assessment of work requirements, open escape routes* and *close proximity to reward*.

Lack of time creates procrastination as students try to prioritise work, social life and university. Strategies to prioritise also lead to working smartly and occasionally procrastination is smarter than doing academic tasks that are not urgent. Some students even procrastinate as a way of building up to getting to work. The open escape routes spoken of are ways to alleviate the negative feelings associated with procrastination: feeling guilty or lazy, for example. Also, they would sometimes procrastinate because they preferred doing work at the last minute and getting feedback relatively quickly than handing in assignments early only to have to then wait a very long time for a response after the deadline. Together, these emerging factors help to explain students' behaviours around procrastination. What is interesting is that this comes remarkably close to the themes one might imagine emerging from an interpretative phenomenological analysis. Together, the themes form a model that is really rather close to explaining the lived experience of the student. The difference mostly lies in the level of interpretation that has occurred. Because this is grounded theory, interpretation is much less important and, arguably, consciously avoided.

Source: Schraw, G., Wadkins, T,. & Olafson, L. (2007). Doing the things we do: A grounded theory study of academic procrastination. *Journal of Educational Psychology, 99*, 12–25.

Interpretative phenomenological analysis

Interpretative phenomenological analysis (IPA) is the most 'modern' method and is the method of choice for most health psychologists. It was invented, if that is the correct word to use, by Jonathan Smith and colleagues (1999).

The purpose of IPA is to try to capture how a person makes sense of something around them or their own behaviour. It is interpretative because, of course, we recognise that all human endeavour and attempts at understanding involve interpretation. Interpretation is inescapable. You only experience something as an interpretation, not as it truly might be. It is phenomenological because it is an attempt to put a person's world into perspective and to reflect that viewpoint. No one operates in isolation. They are a living, thinking, feeling person. This means that, in order to get a grasp of a phenomenon, we have to understand phenomenology, or 'lived experience'. IPA is a way of trying to explore what something 'feels like' for a person.

You begin with a systematic search for themes. This is not very different from looking for codes of themes in other types of analysis. You then look for connections between themes and start to look for these across individuals. These themes are refined by further reading. The important thing is to try to stand back from your own experience and so use the text as a means of accessing what the world of the interviewee is like. It doesn't matter what makes sense to you, but what makes sense for your interviewees. Furthermore, the method is not prescribed; you can adapt your method of analysis as long as you keep to the crucial principle of interpretative phenomenology.

The value of qualitative approaches

Qualitative research, it is argued, adds something to our *understanding* of the world. This is a key point. 'Understanding' is a word many qualitative psychologists would use rather than 'knowledge'. Knowledge implies that things we have learned are somehow true, whereas qualitative psychologists would mostly argue truth is relative, holds only for a given person in a given circumstance, and is not generalisable to others at different times in different places. Whilst this can also be a criticism, the realisation of this is considered to be a strength of qualitative research, as is the depth of understanding achieved. Most surveys take the form of rather brief questionnaires, with set questions. Most experimental studies involve tightly predefined measurements of physical behaviours or tendencies, such as reaction time or verbal fluency. Qualitative work, relying as it does mostly on interview or textual analysis, does not presuppose things about the respondent. Instead, the researcher works with what is provided. This means that the respondent is empowered, respected and allowed to express themselves properly.

Further reading Qualitative methods

Topic	Key reading
Thematic analysis	Boyatzis, R. (1998). *Transforming qualitative information: Thematic analysis and code development.* Thousand Oaks, CA: Sage.
Discourse analysis	Potter, J. (1996). *Representing reality: Discourse, rhetoric and social construction.* London: Sage
Grounded theory	Skodol-Wilson, H. & Ambler-Hutchinson, S. (1996). Methodological mistakes in grounded theory. *Nursing Research, 45,* 122–124.
Interpretative phenomenological analysis	Smith, J., & Osborn, M. (2003). Interpretative phenomenological analysis. In J. Smith (Ed.), *Qualitative Psychology: A practical guide to research methods.* London: Sage.

? *Sample question*   *Assessment*

Choose a newspaper article on a contentious topic such as teenage pregnancy or drug-taking and conduct a discourse analysis on the text. Then conduct a thematic analysis and compare your results for the two.

Criticisms of qualitative psychology

As you would imagine, most criticisms of qualitative psychology come from the 'scientist' psychologists. Their view is that qualitative psychology is all very interesting, but not really heading anywhere and is essentially riddled with problems and challenges. To them, it is not science – and psychology should be a science. The strongest view expressed in this respect is essentially that qualitative research is 'a waste of time and good money'.

Particular criticisms can be attached to certain approaches and methods more than others, as follows.

Criticisms of thematic analysis

Thematic analysis is often described as too simple, often failing to capture the richness that one normally associates with qualitative work. Whilst it is often perfectly acceptable for work within other social sciences, it can be too basic for the kinds of issues that psychologists are particularly interested in.

Criticisms of discourse analysis

Discourse analysis is sometimes thought of as a method best suited to critical or social constructionist psychology, but which stops short of what many psychologists need of qualitative research. Discourse analysts are opposed to the view that texts have a meaning per se or *contain* a meaning. Rather, the meaning is *constructed* by the reader. However, for some people this takes away the entire point of conducting an analysis. If all I get from an analysis is what I put into it, then what I produce isn't really telling me anything about the text or the interviewees. Instead, it teaches me things about myself. Of course, if the purpose of my research is to understand teenage mothers, knowing about myself doesn't really help much. I want to know about *them*, not what I think about them myself. If I do truly believe that there is something to understand in a text, a *real* meaning if you like, discourse analysis is not necessarily the way to approach that.

Criticisms of grounded theory

One of the first criticisms of grounded theory is that it is simply impossible to start your research with a blank slate, as it were. The idea that someone should allow the theories to somehow emerge from the data cannot occur in a 'pure' fashion. If a person is interested enough in a subject to want to research it, they are probably already partly knowledgeable in the area and have possibly read a good number of related articles. They are also likely to have various suppositions and prejudices about the topic being researched from the outset, which they would bring to the process of data collection. It is simply impossible for a human being to be 'empty' of ideas, hypotheses, hunches and theories when they begin. The supporters of grounded theory say that they accept this, but the aim is to start *as close as possible* to empty.

Criticisms of interpretative phenomenological analysis

The main criticisms of IPA come from other approaches, because, for example, IPA does allow for some interpretation leading to an ultimate aim of understanding the world of the participant. Discourse analysts would argue you simply cannot do that and to try is disingenuous. Others would also argue that, by setting out your interpretation of someone else's experience, you take their own voice away. In other words, the transcripts should 'speak for themselves'.

Test your knowledge

9.4 List three main criticisms of qualitative methods as used in psychology.

An answer to this question can be found on the companion website at: **www.pearsoned.co.uk/psychologyexpress**

? *Sample question*   *Essay*

Two what extent does qualitative research solve all of the problems associated with quantitative research?

Chapter summary – pulling it all together

→ Can you tick all the points from the revision checklist at the beginning of this chapter?

→ Attempt the sample question from the beginning of this chapter using the answer guidelines overleaf.

→ Go to the companion website at www.pearsoned.co.uk/psychologyexpress to access more revision support online, including interactive quizzes, flashcards, You be the marker exercises as well as answer guidance for the Test your knowledge and Sample questions from this chapter.

Further reading for Chapter 9	
Topic	Key reading
Thematic analysis: theory and practice	Boyatzis, R. (1998). *Transforming qualitative information: Thematic analysis and code development.* Thousand Oaks, CA: Sage.

Answer guidelines

 Sample question Essay

> What is the value of qualitative research? Illustrate your answer with reference to two approaches.

Approaching the question

You must first of all read the question. The question asks for two approaches to be used to demonstrate value. Firstly, think carefully about which approaches you choose to discuss. Choose those you know about and which together form a good pair. Don't choose two very similar ones because you will have less to say overall. Furthermore, the question asks for the 'value' of qualitative research. In order to explain what the value is, arguably you can also talk about what's wrong with it. Together the two sides of the story make up the value.

Important points to include

- Begin your answer by setting out which two approaches you are using to illustrate the value of qualitative research.

- Then you could choose, perhaps, to demonstrate value by selecting half a dozen criticisms of quantitative research, taking each in turn and explaining why qualitative approaches are better. For example, the lack of depth often reported in quantitative studies can be addressed by the richer, deeper analysis that qualitative approaches usually yield.

- Then, you might wish to take some criticisms of the qualitative approach and give counter-answers for those. So, for example, the fact that qualitative work is all about interpretation can be turned around into a positive thing, given it is valuable for us to explicitly recognise the human interpretative contribution we make in analysis data and constructing science. Therefore, you could argue that qualitative research is more 'honest'.

- Finish off by summarising your arguments and leave one good point to the end, which will strengthen the answer and leave the reader impressed by your understanding. The section below on making your answer stand out gives you an example of such a final point.

Make your answer stand out

To get the best possible marks, try to ensure that you show a deep understanding of the issues in qualitative exploration, including the very challenge to the concept of value that many qualitative approaches involve. Make it clear that what qualitative researchers call value isn't the same as what their quantitative counterparts would.

Explore the accompanying website at www.pearsoned.co.uk/psychologyexpress
→ Prepare more effectively for exams and assignments using the answer guidelines for questions from this chapter.
→ Test your knowledge using multiple choice questions and flashcards.
→ Improve your essay skills by exploring the You be the marker exercises.

Notes

Notes

Ethics of research with humans and animals

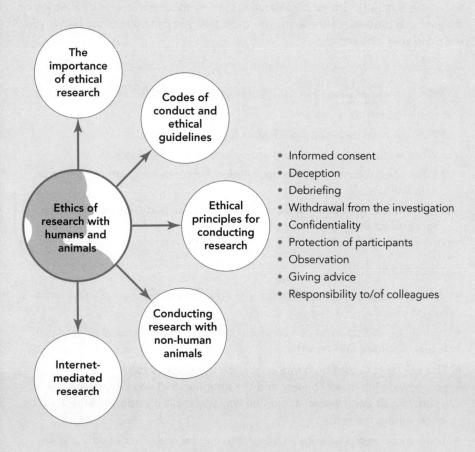

- Informed consent
- Deception
- Debriefing
- Withdrawal from the investigation
- Confidentiality
- Protection of participants
- Observation
- Giving advice
- Responsibility to/of colleagues

A printable version of this topic map is available from
www.pearsoned.co.uk/psychologyexpress

Introduction

It is essential that you have a good understanding of ethical issues in psychological research. This means that you must be able to explain why codes of conduct and ethics are necessary in psychological research, as well as identify and discuss examples of the ethical issues that may arise. It is very important that you remember codes of conduct and ethical guidelines for psychologists are not intended to be exhaustive checklists specifying precisely what can and cannot be done. The crucial aspect of understanding research ethics is that you appreciate the importance of thinking about each research study as an individual case and can show you can do this. There is much more to having a good grasp of research ethics than remembering a list of principles and applying them as a checklist in a very superficial way. Ethical considerations are all about thinking and reflecting on the research process, so the more you show that you can do this, the better you will do in your assessments.

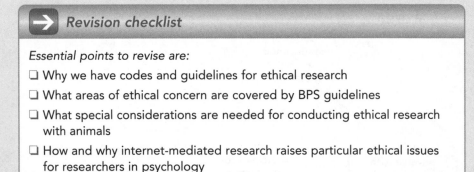

→ Revision checklist

Essential points to revise are:

❏ Why we have codes and guidelines for ethical research

❏ What areas of ethical concern are covered by BPS guidelines

❏ What special considerations are needed for conducting ethical research with animals

❏ How and why internet-mediated research raises particular ethical issues for researchers in psychology

Assessment advice

- Your knowledge and understanding of ethical issues in psychological research can be assessed in a number of ways.

- You will be expected to demonstrate the application of ethical principles in research studies and reports.

- This will be reflected both in the way you design your study (e.g. how you provide informed consent and the attention that you pay to effective debriefing of participants) and in the way you explicitly address ethical issues when writing the report.

- You may be asked to write an essay focusing on one or more ethical issue, or you may have to answer a problem-based exam question in which you discuss the major issues or apply them to a real or hypothetical situation or research study.

- Make sure that you have a broad understanding of ethical principles and how to apply them, beyond a simple 'checklist' approach.

Sample question

Could you answer this question? Below is a typical essay question that could arise on this topic.

 Sample question *Essay*

Critically discuss whether it is justifiable to deceive participants in research studies.

Guidelines on answering this question are included at the end of this chapter, whilst further guidance on tackling other exam questions can be found on the companion website at: **www.pearsoned.co.uk/psychologyexpress**

The importance of ethical research

The importance of conducting psychological research ethically is really a matter of making sure that participants are treated properly. Psychological research most commonly involves the direct participation of people, the majority of whom may not know much about psychology or psychologists. These are significant considerations for the following main reasons.

- At a fundamental level, we must recognise that psychologists do not have a special right to treat other human beings however they want to, in the name of 'research'.

- There is a real potential for causing harm or offence to people if we do not carefully consider the possible consequences of the tasks, questions and experiences to which we expose participants.

- The researcher may be in a position of real or perceived power in relation to the participants.

- The reputation of psychology and psychologists depends very much upon the experiences that participants have when they take part in research. Without the voluntary contribution of participants, there would be no research and psychology would not be able to advance knowledge of human behaviour.

Test your knowledge

10.1 Why do we need to have codes of ethics for research? What purpose do they serve?

An answer to this question can be found on the companion website at: **www.pearsoned.co.uk/psychologyexpress**

Codes of conduct and ethical guidelines

The British Psychological Society (BPS) publishes a range of documents that together provide a clear set of principles by which professional psychologists are expected to conduct themselves in their dealings with their clients or research participants. These are not rules and regulations, but guidelines that psychologists should strive to adhere to in their professional lives. The BPS *Code of ethics and conduct*, the latest version of which was published in August 2009, sets out four major ethical principles covering the main areas of responsibility within which more specific ethical issues are covered. The four major principles are defined in Table 10.1.

Table 10.1 BPS ethical principles

Principle	BPS statement of values
Respect	Psychologists value the dignity and worth of all persons, with sensitivity to the dynamics of perceived authority or influence over clients and with particular regard to people's rights, including those of privacy and self-determination.
Competence	Psychologists value the continuing development and maintenance of high standards of competence in their professional work and the importance of preserving their ability to function optimally within the recognised limits of their knowledge, skill, training, education and experience.
Responsibility	Psychologists value their responsibilities to clients, to the general public and to the profession and science of psychology, including the avoidance of harm and the prevention of misuse or abuse of their contributions to society.
Integrity	Psychologists value honesty, accuracy, clarity and fairness in their interactions with all persons and seek to promote integrity in all facets of their scientific and professional endeavours.

These four broad principles are intended to apply to all aspects of psychological work, including both practitioners and researchers. More specific guidelines for conducting research are provided in the BPS *Ethical principles for conducting research with human participants*.

Test your knowledge

10.2 What are the four principles listed in the BPS *Code of ethics and conduct*? Can you explain what each one means?

Answers to these questions can be found on the companion website at:
www.pearsoned.co.uk/psychologyexpress

Ethical principles for conducting research

The BPS provides a set of nine main areas of concern for conducting research in psychology. These are shown in Figure 10.1. It is easy to learn these areas of concern as a list, but it is vital to appreciate that the issues raised by some of them can be very complex and require some sophisticated and critical analysis when applying them to an individual research study.

Informed consent

Wherever possible, the researcher must obtain informed consent from the participants, which involves providing them with full information about the objectives of the research. It is important that participants have a full understanding of all of the aspects of the study that would be expected to influence their willingness to participate. This will, at the very least, mean that participants must know at the outset what type of thing they are expected to do, how long it will take and so on.

There are special considerations to be made for participants who may have limited understanding (e.g. children or individuals with mental impairments).

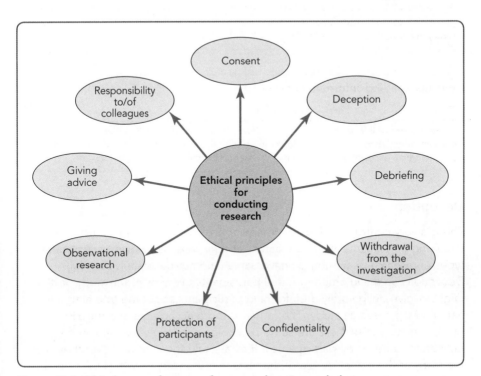

Figure 10.1 **Ethical areas of concern for researchers in psychology**

The researcher must emphasise the voluntary nature of the participation and must be aware of any position of authority or power relationship that may influence potential participants and result in people feeling coerced to 'volunteer'.

Participants can give informed consent by signing a form or a letter or, in the case of questionnaire studies, it is implied by their completion and return of the questionnaire.

CRITICAL FOCUS

Student participation in research

It is common practice in universities in the USA for students to be required to participate in research studies in order to gain course credits. In the UK, this requirement is becoming more common and the BPS (2004) recognises that participation provides valuable experience and it would be unethical for psychology students or graduates to carry out research with others unless they themselves had been willing to participate in research. The BPS (2004: 8) suggests, '...it is recommended that participants should be given alternatives so that there is no coercion to participate in any *particular* study' and '...where research participation is a course requirement, that this be clearly stated in the course handbooks or other advertising material, enabling prospective students that do not wish to take part in research to opt for a different course'.

Imagine that a student enrols on a psychology degree programme, fully aware that some research participation will be required, yet, when it comes to it, does not feel they wish to participate in any of the studies on offer at the time. What ethical issues does this raise?

Further reading Informed consent

Topic	Key reading
Is the process of informed consent effective in psychological experiments?	Brody, J., Gluck, J., & Aragon, A. (1997). Participants' understanding of the process of psychological research: Informed consent. *Ethics & Behavior, 7*(4), 285–298.

Deception

This is a very controversial issue. Wherever possible, researchers must avoid deceiving participants about the nature of their research. However, for some types of research deception is unavoidable (and not necessarily harmful). Deception can mean omitting to tell participants the aims of the study or it might involve deliberately misinforming participants about the true aims and nature of the research study. The former is more acceptable and the BPS guidelines recognise there are some psychological processes that can be deliberately altered by participants if they are told the aims and hypotheses of the study at the outset. A rule of thumb is that the withholding of information or the misleading of participants is unacceptable if the participants are typically likely to object or show unease once debriefed. If there is any doubt, as with all ethical issues, the researcher must consult with disinterested colleagues about the suitability of the deception. Whenever any form of deception is used, the full information must be provided to participants at the earliest opportunity.

Further reading Deception	
Topic	Key reading
The justification of deception	Bortolotti, L., & Mameli, M. (2006). Deception in psychology: Moral costs and benefits of unsought self-knowledge. *Accountability in Research: Policies & Quality Assurance, 13*(3), 259–275.
Argument against deception	Oliansky, A. (1991). A confederate's perspective on deception. *Ethics & Behavior, 1*(4), 253–258.
Role-play as an alternative method	Mixon, D. (1972). Instead of deception. *Journal for the Theory of Social Behaviour, 2*(2), 145–177.
An overview and evaluation of experimental deception in psychology	Hertwig, R., & Ortmann, A. (2008). Deception in experiments: Revisiting the arguments in its defense. *Ethics & Behavior, 18*(1), 59–92.

Debriefing

After the data have been collected, participants must be informed of the full nature of the research. This involves more than simply telling them what the research is about. There must be an active intervention to ensure that participants leave the research in the same state they were in when they entered. Any harmful consequences must be removed (e.g. if a negative mood state has been induced as part of an experiment, then a more positive mood state must be induced before the participant leaves the study). The debriefing is an opportunity to further explore how the participant feels about the research experience and to correct any misconceptions that they might have about the research and its aims. It is also an important time to offer an explicit opportunity to participants to withdraw from the study. They may not, for example, feel happy about the way that an interview went or perhaps they said some things that, on reflection, they would rather not have included in the study. It is also important to ensure that the participant fully understands what you are going to do with the data. Debriefing is not a justification for any unethical aspects of the research.

Further reading Debriefing	
Topic	Key reading
Effectiveness of experimental debriefing with children	Hurley, J., & Underwood, M. (2002). Children's understanding of their research rights before and after debriefing: Informed assent, confidentiality, and stopping participation. *Child Development, 73*(1), 132–143.

Withdrawal from the investigation

The BPS guidelines state that researchers should inform participants they have the right to withdraw from the study at any time, and this includes the right to withdraw consent retrospectively and to request their data be destroyed. This is one aspect of the ethical principles that merits further consideration. Typically, the right to 'withdraw at any time' is understood by students and incorporated into participant information sheets and task instructions for research studies, but it is important to reflect on what limitations must be placed on this in practical terms. For example, participants cannot withdraw their data if the study has already been published.

CRITICAL FOCUS

The adherence to ethical principles

It is, of course, important to ensure that studies are conducted ethically, but difficulties can arise in regard to some of the principles, as the following illustrate.

- If data are collected anonymously (e.g. through a computer-controlled experiment), it might be impossible for the participant to subsequently withdraw from the study, as their data would not be identifiable.

- In the case of data collected via group discussions, the researcher cannot guarantee confidentiality, as participants may disclose what was said during the discussion to others afterwards.

- The withdrawal of an individual's data from, for example, the transcript of a group discussion may also render the contributions of other participants meaningless (if, for example, participant Y's statements only make sense in light of what participant X said just beforehand, then participant X's withdrawal might mean that participant Y is also effectively withdrawn, thus wasting their time).

The key to these issues is to ensure that all participants are fully informed of what might happen, and, crucially, to think all of these possibilities through when devising the research study. This, again, demonstrates why research ethics involves much more than box-ticking.

Confidentiality

Participants can expect their participation in the study and any other information provided by them to be kept confidential unless otherwise agreed. If the study is published then the identities of the participants must be protected (again, unless agreed). Note that issues of anonymity are typically more central to research than confidentiality. Researchers must be able to report what was said and done, but take care not to allow participants to be identified. Issues of confidentiality are more central to therapeutic practice, where nothing that a client says should be revealed, whether anonymously or otherwise. If there is a danger that anonymity may not be possible in a research study, then participants should be warned of this from the outset.

The commitment to anonymity can be at odds with the aims of some qualitative research, which is to give participants a 'voice'. It may also portray people as powerless and needing to be protected by the 'powerful' researcher.

Protection of participants

Participants must be protected from both physical and mental harm during the research. Participants should not be exposed to any risk greater than they would normally face. This includes the protection of participant privacy, e.g. researching very sensitive topics, which could be construed as an invasion of privacy. Some research situations may encourage revelations that distress the participant, so anticipating and responding sensitively to emotional responses is vital. While 'upset' is not necessarily the same as 'harm', mishandling by the researcher can make it so. The researcher must be prepared for what might happen; having experience or working with someone who has experience of this type of research is crucial.

Observation

Studies based on observational methods cannot enforce several of the ethical guidelines (e.g. informed consent, full debriefing), which raises the problem of *involuntary participation*. In such cases, researchers should respect the privacy of participants. Observation should only occur in situations where people would expect to be observed, taking into account local and cultural norms.

 Sample question   *Assessment*

Laud Humprheys and the 'tearoom trade'

Laud Humphreys (1970) was interested in learning about the motives of individuals who engage in sexual acts in public toilets (referred to as 'tearooms'). To this end, Humphreys staked-out public amenities where homosexual men were known to gather for the purpose of engaging in sexual behaviours. These illegal encounters usually involved two men who participated in the sex act and a third man – or 'watchqueen' – who raised the alarm when a police car or a stranger approached. Humphreys volunteered to serve as watchqueen so that he could observe hundreds of impersonal sexual acts. In some cases, Humphreys was able to persuade some of the men he observed to give him information about their personal lives and their motives. In other instances, he recorded the number plate details of the men's cars in the toilet car park and then obtained their addresses from the department of public safety. Later, while wearing a disguise, he would claim to be a health service employee and visit their homes for the purpose of interviewing them about their marital status, occupation, etc.

Source: Humphreys, L. (1970). *Tearoom trade: A study of homosexual encounters in public places*. London: Duckworth.

1 What ethical issues are raised by this research?

2 Could the study's objectives have been achieved by other (ethical) means?

Giving advice

In certain situations, researchers may become aware of a physical or psychological problem that a participant is unaware of. The researcher has a responsibility to inform the participant and provide/recommend appropriate help and advice. The researcher should not give advice on matters about which they are unqualified to deal. In these circumstances they should refer the participant to the appropriate source of professional advice. In interview situations on some topic areas, it is important to be very careful that the participant does not misconstrue the interview situation as an opportunity for 'therapy'.

Responsibility to/of colleagues

Investigators share responsibility for maintaining high ethical standards in their research and should monitor their own work and that of others. Sharing responsibility in this way helps protect the reputation of psychology as a science and the well-being of psychological participants. A psychologist who believes that a colleague's work is unethical should encourage that colleague to re-think their methods.

The sharing of responsibility is enshrined in the notion that no research study should ever be conducted without having been reviewed and approved by an ethics committee.

Test your knowledge

10.3 What are the nine areas of concern listed in the BPS *Ethical principles for conducting research with human participants?* Can you explain each one and give examples?

An answer to this question can be found on the companion website at: **www.pearsoned.co.uk/psychologyexpress**

CRITICAL FOCUS

Milgram's (1963) experiments on obedience

Stanley Milgram's experimental studies of obedience are among the most cited and discussed in psychology, particularly in reference to ethics. You are probably familiar with these experiments, but, just in case you are not, Milgram deceived participants into believing that they were administering painful electric shocks to another participant. The severity of the 'shocks' increased as the experiment progressed and were accompanied by pre-recorded screams and shouts from the apparent 'victim'. Participants who expressed doubts, or even displayed signs of severe mental anguish, about continuing were told that they must do so by the experimenter. Milgram found that 65 per cent of participants completed the experiment and administered the maximum 450-volt shock. Having consulted widely on the predicted outcomes prior to conducting the study, Milgram was surprised by the results, as psychiatrists had predicted that only 0.1 per cent of participants would obey the experimenter's instructions and continue to the end of the experiment. Milgram's famously interpreted his findings as demonstrating that ordinary people can, when under pressure, perform acts that would ordinarily be considered cruel or inhuman.

Source: Milgram, S. (1983). Behavioral study of obedience. *The Journal of Abnormal and Social Psychology, 67*(4), 371–378.

 Sample question   *Assessment*

1 What aspects of Milgram's experiments do you think were unethical?
2 Do you think that the outcomes and psychological effects on participants were predictable?
3 Would the impact that Milgram's experiments have made on research ethics in psychology have been as significant had his participants refused to deliver any electric shocks at all? To what extent do you think that this matters?

Conducting research with non-human animals

The use of animals in research is an extremely controversial and emotive issue. There are those who object in principle to the use of animals in any form of research, whether it is medical or psychological. Others believe that some animal research is both necessary and justified and the benefits outweigh the costs to the individual animals.

Putting the broader debate aside, there are specific ethical issues around the use of animals in psychological research. Animals cannot provide informed consent, withdraw from the research or be debriefed, so the use of animals in research is regulated very tightly by the 1986 Animals (Scientific Procedures) Act. The BPS (2007) *Guidelines for psychologists working with animals* remind psychologists of 'their general obligation to avoid or at least minimise discomfort to living animals'. The 1986 Animals Act covers all non-human vertebrates as well as the invertebrate *Octopus vulgaris* (the common octopus). Other invertebrates are not covered, but the BPS guidelines suggest that psychologists should aim to maintain the same standards in all animal research. Any procedure that may cause pain, suffering, distress or lasting harm to an animal is covered by the 1986 Animal Act and the researcher must be licensed in order to undertake this type of research.

Psychologists are required to:

- comply with all applicable laws regarding animal welfare
- choose a species that will suffer the least while meeting the scientific objectives of the research
- use the smallest number of animals sufficient to accomplish the research goals
- consider employing experimental procedures that enhance or enrich the animal's environment rather than have a negative impact
- house animals in conditions least likely to cause distress or harm, with due regard to the needs of animals of different species, age, sex, social status and so on.

Researchers observing the behaviour of free-living animals should take precautions to minimise interference to the environment or to individual animals or groups.

Further reading **Conducting research with non-human animals**

Topic	Key reading
BPS guidelines	BPS (2007). *Guidelines for psychologists working with animals.* Leicester: British Psychological Society
Field experiments	Cuthill, I. (1991). Field experiments in animal behaviour: Methods and ethics. *Animal Behaviour, 42,* 1007–1014.

Test your knowledge

10.4 Why is it necessary to have additional ethical guidelines for research involving non-human animals?

10.5 What types of animals are covered by the 1986 Animals (Scientific Procedures) Act?

10.6 What special considerations must psychologists allow for when planning animal research?

Answers to these questions can be found on the companion website at: **www.pearsoned.co.uk/psychologyexpress**

Internet-mediated research

The internet provides a wealth of opportunity for psychologists to undertake research in many different ways, including online experiments, questionnaire studies, interviews and the observation of behaviour in chat rooms or discussion groups. Although online surveys and experiments can be a very efficient way of collecting data, there are some specific ethical issues raised by *internet-mediated research*.

Participants may be recruited to take part or they may be unaware that they are being observed (if, for example, their contributions to a discussion forum are being analysed). Further, participants might be identifiable as individuals or they may be anonymous. The absence of face-to-face contact between researcher and participant makes it difficult for the researcher to verify the identity of the participant, to monitor the effects that the study may have or to intervene effectively if participants express negative outcomes of participating. Debriefing can be much more difficult, as can issues around withdrawal from the study. If, for example, a participant stops responding to questions, does it mean that they have withdrawn completely or would they be happy with their responses up to that point being used?

The unobtrusive observation of online activity in discussion groups or similar websites raises complex questions about the distinction between public and private spaces, whether this type of activity constitutes deception and the extent to which the reporting of the study might lead to individuals being identifiable. Could, for example, particular phrases and statements be found and individuals identified through a simple Google search?

Further reading Internet-mediated research	
Topic head	*Key reading*
Conducting research on the internet	BPS (2007). *Report of the working party on conducting research on the internet: Guidelines for ethical practice in psychological research online.* Leicester: British Psychological Society.
Securing informed consent	Rosser, B., Gurak, L., Horvath, K., Oakes, J., Konstan, J., & Danilenko, G. (2009). The challenges of ensuring participant consent in internet-based sex studies: A case study of the men's INTernet sex (MINTS-I and II) studies. *Journal of Computer-Mediated Communication, 14*(3), 602–626.
The US perspective	Barchard, K., & Williams, J. (2008). Practical advice for conducting ethical online experiments and questionnaires for United States psychologists. *Behavior Research Methods, 40*(4), 1111–1128.

Test your knowledge

10.7 What is the fundamental difference between traditional research in psychology and the use of the internet to conduct research?

10.8 What ethical issues are raised particularly by the use of the internet to conduct research?

Answers to these questions can be found on the companion website at:
www.pearsoned.co.uk/psychologyexpress

 Sample question   *Essay*

Discuss the ethical issues raised by internet-mediated research in psychology. How and to what extent can they be resolved?

Chapter summary – pulling it all together

→ Can you tick all the points from the revision checklist at the beginning of this chapter?

→ Attempt the sample question from the beginning of this chapter using the answer guidelines below.

→ Go to the companion website at www.pearsoned.co.uk/psychologyexpress to access more revision support online, including interactive quizzes, flashcards, You be the marker exercises as well as answer guidance for the Test your knowledge and Sample questions from this chapter.

Further reading for Chapter 10

Topic	Key reading
BPS code of ethics	BPS (2009). *Code of ethics and conduct*. Leicester: British Psychological Society.
Deception	Mixon, D. (1974). If you won't deceive, what can you do? In N. Armistead (Ed.), *Reconstructing social psychology*. London: Penguin Education.

Answer guidelines

 Sample question   *Essay*

Critically discuss whether it is justifiable to deceive participants in research studies.

Approaching the question

- The question asks you to critically discuss whether it is justifiable to deceive participants in research studies.
- Take a critical and discursive approach; there is no 'correct answer'.
- It is essential to show that you have carefully considered all of the key points and you have read around the subject.

Important points to include

- The starting point for this question would be to define and discuss what is considered to be 'deception', how the BPS codes and guidelines define it and what they say about it. The case for and against the use of deception can be constructed by drawing on famous examples, such as the Asch studies of conformity and Milgram's obedience studies, but also the more recent discussions provided in the 'Further reading' box earlier in this chapter and any number of studies from psychology that have used mild forms of deception.
- Pay attention to the potential link between deception, psychological harm and the use of debriefing. Consider whether the BPS guidelines address this sufficiently; you might, for instance, consider the difficulties involved in anticipating whether participants are likely to be distressed or offended once the deception is revealed.
- Consider the effect deception can have on participants' impressions of psychology and psychologists and discuss the potential damage that can be done to the discipline and further research if deception is over-used.

> **Make your answer stand out**
>
> *The use of deception in psychological studies is a very contentious issue. The key to making your answer stand out is to emphasise that the application of ethics codes is a matter of judgement and researchers in psychology should always consult disinterested colleagues when planning research. There are some suggested alternatives to deception and a discussion of the adequacy of these, weighed against the perceived benefits of avoiding deception, would make your answer stand out. Try to avoid presenting 'standard' criticisms of, for example, Milgram's studies. Show you are aware that ethical codes and practices change over time and, although Milgram's studies would not be ethically acceptable now, the times were different in the early 1960s. Base your*

discussion and conclusions on a careful and thorough reading of a wide range of sources, covering all of the key aspects. If you can use your own examples of research to illustrate your points, this will help.

Explore the accompanying website at www.pearsoned.co.uk/psychologyexpress

→ Prepare more effectively for exams and assignments using the answer guidelines for questions from this chapter.

→ Test your knowledge using multiple choice questions and flashcards.

→ Improve your essay skills by exploring the You be the marker exercises.

Notes

Reporting research

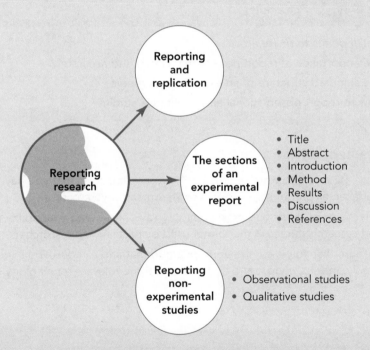

Introduction

Reporting research is a key activity for all researchers in psychology and it is crucial that those engaged with the study of psychology are able to communicate their ideas clearly and unambiguously. In short, there must be a shared understanding, not just of the underlying principles of research methods in psychology, but also of the ways in which the outcomes of research studies will be reported. The adoption of a consistent approach ensures some standardisation of the way in which information will be communicated and so helps to avoid confusion or misunderstanding. It is important that you understand the basic structure, organisation and content of this consistent approach so that you, too, are able to report and summarise research findings clearly and accurately.

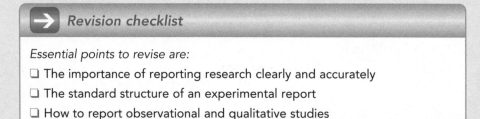

→ Revision checklist

Essential points to revise are:

❏ The importance of reporting research clearly and accurately
❏ The standard structure of an experimental report
❏ How to report observational and qualitative studies

Assessment advice

- You will be asked to write reports on the research studies that you have undertaken as part of the practical work element of your course.

- This is the most direct and most common way of assessing your ability to report research studies in the format used by professional researchers.

- Make sure that you know the appropriate format and can describe studies precisely, making correct and accurate use of the relevant terminology.

Reporting and replication

The whole point of writing a report is to provide an account of a study that has been conducted. The intended audience for a research report is the 'educated stranger'. That is, someone who understands the general principles of psychology and its associated methods of research but who does not, prior to reading the report, have any knowledge of what the study entailed. The information contained in the report must be sufficiently detailed to allow this educated stranger to understand exactly what has been done, what has been found and what the author of the report thinks the findings mean.

The purpose of providing this detail is to allow an equivalent study to be conducted in order to test the theory further. In Chapters 1 and 2, the scientific methods of psychology were discussed, so you should already appreciate how and why the advancement of psychological knowledge depends very much on a clear understanding of what research has already been done and what has been found. The replication of effects is central to the development of psychology as a discipline and it is the clear and accurate reporting of research studies and their findings that is essential for this.

The following sections of this chapter will focus on the structure and content of the typical experimental report. The variations that are necessary for reporting other types of study will be discussed later on.

The sections of an experimental report

Title

This is not really a 'section' as such, but every report needs to begin with a title. An ideal title is short and to the point. Titles like 'A Psychology Experiment' are very unhelpful. Similarly, the title 'An Experiment to Find Whether Participants in One Condition Asked to Answer a Series of Questions Would Answer the Final Question Differently from Another Group of Participants Asked Just a Single Question' is far too long-winded. The title should be a 10–15-word description of what the experiment involved and should make reference to the independent variable(s) and the dependent variable(s). For example, 'Effects of Eating Strawberries or Parsnips on Memory for Words' refers to the independent variable (the type of food eaten) and the dependent variable (memory for words).

Abstract

The abstract is a short summary of the entire report, designed to help the reader decide whether they want to read the entire report or not. Abstracts that are misleading can be very frustrating to the reader if it turns out that, for example, the conclusions drawn at the end of the report are not quite the same as stated in the abstract. Abstracts should be no longer than about 100–200 words and should say what was done in the study, what was found and what this means. There should not be too much detail, but there should be enough information for the reader to understand exactly what the study entailed and what the main findings were.

Introduction

The 'Introduction' section is where the rationale for the study is explained. The main purpose of the introduction is to explain why your study has been developed and how it fits in with previous research studies and their findings. By the end of the introduction, the reader should find that they understand what the study is about, how it relates to other studies and why a particular outcome was expected from the study. It is important to remember that you are presenting an argument, which needs to be coherent and logical. The introduction has the same general format and purpose for every type of study, whether it is an experiment, a questionnaire study or a qualitative study (but note that qualitative research deals with research aims and research questions rather than hypotheses and expectations).

You will be describing other research studies that you have read about and are relevant to your study.

Overall, the content of the introduction must reflect the rationale for the study and set out all of your reasoning. These considerations are set out in Chapters 1 and 2 of this book, so it is worth cross-checking to make sure that you are describing the development and background of your study properly.

CRITICAL FOCUS

Constructing an introduction

Students sometimes miss the point of the introduction section and lose sight of the fact that it is a detailed explanation of what the study is based on and the reasons it was designed. It may be helpful to think of the introduction as a mini-essay. Imagine that the title is: 'Explain, with reference to relevant research, why your study was designed, what its aims were and (for quantitative studies) what you expected to find and why'.

Avoid falling into the common trap of just describing several studies and then presenting your hypothesis. Explain how each previous study or theory informed yours and provide a clear account of how this led to the design of your study. Don't forget to provide an explicit explanation of your hypotheses and how and why they were developed.

Method

The method section is a concise description of how the study was conducted and should strike a balance between detail and brevity. There should be enough information for someone to replicate your study, but irrelevant details should be omitted. The method section for experimental studies is usually subdivided into the following sections:

- design
- participants
- apparatus/materials
- procedure.

Present them in whatever order provides the clearest account of the method. It usually makes sense, however, for the Procedure to be at the end; this leads logically into the results and an account of the procedure doesn't really make much sense unless the materials and the design have been explained. Note that your research methods tutor may have their own preference for the order of the subsections of the method section, so please double-check what they prefer you to do.

Design

In this section of an experimental report, the independent and dependent variables should be stated and defined clearly. Write whether the independent variables were manipulated between- or within-groups, i.e. was the experiment a between-groups design, a within-groups design or a mixed design? Write how many levels there were of each independent variable and explain the levels of variables clearly.

CRITICAL FOCUS

Defining variables

'The independent variable was the film and the dependent variable was score.' This brief, largely uninformative statement is a fairly common occurrence in experimental reports written by students who do not appreciate what is meant by *defining* variables. Make sure that you provide a proper explanation and don't just attempt to provide the reader with a snappy soundbite that doesn't actually tell them what they need to know. Compare the example above with this alternative:

> This was a between-groups design with one independent variable. The independent variable was the type of film that participants watched. This had three levels: comedy, horror and neutral. In the *comedy* condition, a clip from the film *Ghostbusters* was used. In the *horror* condition, a clip from *The Exorcist* was shown. The *neutral* condition included a clip from a documentary about limpets. The dependent variable was the self-rated mood of participants after watching the film.

Note how the conditions are labelled *comedy*, *horror* and *neutral*. Later on in the report, these labels can be used again as a quick-and-easy way of referring to the groups. It is not helpful to the reader to label groups *Group 1*, *Group 2*, or *A* and *B*. Always use meaningful labels, so the reader does not have to keep trying to remember which group was which.

Participants

This section describes:

- who took part
- how they were selected.

Students often have problems with describing the selection process. Do not just say that participants were selected using 'convenience sampling', or 'opportunity sampling', and certainly not 'randomly'. It is more useful to explain,

171

in plain English, exactly what you did to recruit participants. If, for example, you stood outside the library and approached every third person who passed by or approached everyone seated in the students' union bar, then say so. If you asked an entire class of students to participate, then say so. The explanation of what you did is more important than giving it a label.

Report major demographic characteristics, such as gender or age, if they are important to the study. Point out, for example, if all of your participants were male, as this might affect the generalisability of the results. If a particular characteristic is an independent variable or is important for the interpretation of the results, then describe the group specifically. If the participants were divided into groups, write how many were in each group and how, exactly, participants were assigned to conditions. State the population from which the participants were drawn (e.g. first-year psychology students at Trumpton and Chigley University). The nature of the study will determine what other information to report (e.g. the heights of participants would need to be reported if height were an experimental variable).

Apparatus/materials

- 'Apparatus' refers to physical equipment (e.g. projectors, computers, buckets of water) used in the experiment. Some experiments do not use any apparatus. If you have used a piece of apparatus, you must describe it in enough detail for the reader to be able to understand what it looked like, what its main features were and how it was used. It can be very difficult to describe apparatus, so it might be very helpful if you include a clear diagram. Draw a picture of the apparatus to augment your written description.

- 'Materials' refers to experimental stimuli and measures (e.g. word lists, pictures, questionnaires). Give enough information for people reading your report to construct similar, equivalent, stimuli. If you have used a standard questionnaire or test, then give a reference for it. If you want to list all of your stimuli, you may put them in an appendix, but they still must be described in this section. It is not enough to say 'The stimuli were adapted from Bloggs (2008)' or 'The materials consisted of some questions. They are shown in the appendix'. You must *describe* the materials fully.

CRITICAL FOCUS

Describing materials

In some experiments you may have used large numbers of stimuli – for instance, 50 words or 100 pictures. Obviously, presenting them all in your materials section is not really practical. You do, however, need to say how many stimuli there were, what types of stimuli were used and how and why they were selected. If your stimuli are the same as those used by an earlier study, then say so. If your materials are similar to those used by other researchers and you have modified them, you must say how your materials have been modified and how they are different from those used by other researchers.

In all cases, you must describe your materials in enough detail for the reader of your report to be able to construct the same or similar stimuli if they want to. The description and explanation are crucial because a particular finding or psychological phenomenon is not really of much use or interest if it occurs only with a specific set of stimulus materials. It is vital to be able to test that the same findings can be found with *different* stimuli which have the same *characteristics* as those reported, so listing examples without explaining what they are examples of, or why, is not particularly helpful in this regard.

Procedure

Often, a chronological account of what happened to individual participants from the start to the end of their participation is best. Pay attention to detail, but do not include irrelevant information. For example, it is important to say how long participants were given to do whatever they did, but you do not need to say which room the study took place in. If standardised instructions were used, these should be placed in an appendix and *paraphrased* in the procedure section. Do not write the instructions out verbatim (word-for-word). At the other extreme, do not just write 'Standardised instructions were used. These are shown in the appendix'. Report any steps taken to reduce experimental bias (e.g. experimenter effects, practice effects or order effects).

The main point is that the Procedure section should allow anyone reading it to understand what participants in the study were asked to do and what they experienced. A common mistake is to write a Procedure section without saying what participants did. Note that it is not sufficient to say 'The participants then completed the questionnaire', 'The participants then wrote down their answers' or 'The participants made their decision'. You must say exactly what participants did. What questions were they answering? What decision did they have to make? How did they record their responses?

Results

There is little point having conducted a study and made a valuable discovery if it is not clear what you have found and how you have dealt with your data. Ensure that your results section covers the following.

- How were data collated? If the data have been categorised, codified or scored in some way to give a total for each participant, or for each item, you must explain how this was done.

- Provide a concise summary of the data, including an explanation of whether and how any data were excluded from the analysis and for what reasons (e.g. very short or very long response times, participants who did not understand the task properly).

- Provide a summary table or graph. Graphs are useful for presenting complex data where the relationships between different conditions might not be clear from a table of figures, but are not particularly helpful when there are only two means being compared (you don't need a graph to show you that 24 is bigger than 22!) If you present a table or graph, you must make sure that you explain it to the reader. The presentation of tables or graphs is not sufficient on its own.

● Describe your results and tell the reader what to look for in any tables or figures that you have presented. The results should be described briefly and concisely, along with the results of any statistical test.

● Do not include raw data (i.e. individual participants' scores) or any calculations in the results section, unless you have used a non-standard statistical procedure that needs to be explained.

Discussion

After presenting the results, you are in a position to interpret their implications, especially with respect to your original hypothesis or hypotheses. You should begin with a concise summary of your main findings in a few sentences, concentrating on whether or not the results support your original hypothesis. You should not describe all of your findings in great detail: that is what the results section is for. The description of your findings should be followed by an interpretation and discussion of the results in terms of the hypothesis. Say whether the hypothesis was supported or not. The findings should then be discussed in relation to the previous studies that were described in the introduction. It is essential to relate your results to the theories or models that were mentioned in the introduction. Concentrate on explaining what the results might mean and any implications that they might have.

End the discussion with a concluding sentence that sums up your main findings and what they mean in theoretical terms. Overall, remember that the discussion section is intended to be an explanation of your findings in theoretical terms.

CRITICAL FOCUS

Criticising the study's design

Students sometimes get a bit carried away in the discussion with suggesting all kinds of things that might have been 'wrong' with their experiment. Never conclude that the study was badly designed because no significant results were obtained – at most suggest a better-designed study may be required to obtain further evidence. Also, do not talk yourself out of a significant finding, unless you feel that any significant effects you have found *were* caused by problems in the design rather than by the manipulation of the independent variable, *and you can provide a plausible, detailed explanation of this.* Read published journal articles. You will not see researchers arguing that their own significant results are not useful because there were unequal numbers of male and female participants, or the results are not generalisable to the whole world, or it might be because some people were tested on Wednesday and others on Thursday. Researchers concentrate on explaining the theoretical implications of results and considering what the next steps might be in investigating the matter at hand. If you wish to criticise the design of your study, or think that some extraneous variable might have produced your results, you must be able to justify your claims. For example, in an experiment with two conditions, if each group consists of 12 males and 2 females, if there is a difference between the groups on the dependent variable this cannot be explained due to there being more males than females. If, however, one group consisted entirely of males and the other entirely of females, then you might argue that the results could represent a gender difference rather than the effect of the independent variable. Always remember: any flaws that you identify in the design of the study are worthy of mention only if you are able to explain *how* the flaw could be responsible for producing your results.

References

As with all academic writing, the report must have a full set of references presented in a properly formatted references list. Referencing matters for at least three reasons.

- It shows that you have read appropriate material and you know your stuff – the selective and effective use of published sources demonstrates understanding and knowledge.

- It protects you from accidental plagiarism – failing to reference properly can lead to you presenting other people's work as though it is your own.

- References allow your reader to locate and access the original sources if they wish – they might be interested in finding out more about a particular study or, indeed, might want to check whether your interpretation is accurate.

The ability to do this properly is central to meeting the requirements of an academic degree course. There are many guides available on how to reference correctly, but you must ensure the following.

- Are you familiar with the referencing system that is required by your tutor? Most psychology departments in the UK use APA-style referencing.

- Have you made sure that you have included citations to support the points made in your work?

- Have you made sure that you have distinguished between primary and secondary sources?

- Have you made sure that each reference on the references list contains the correct information for the type of reference (e.g. book or journal article)?

- Have you checked that the references list contains *all* of the sources that you have identified in your text as primary sources?

- Have you checked that the references list *only* contains sources that you have identified in your text as primary sources?

Never submit work to be marked unless you can answer 'yes' to all of these questions.

Reporting non-experimental studies

Observational studies

There are different types of observational study and observational data can be analysed quantitatively or qualitatively. The precise information to be included in the method section will, therefore, depend upon the type of study. For quasi-experimental designs, you will need to include a design section in which you describe the variables. In some observational work, you might classify observations into categories. It is important to describe the coding criteria, the types of behaviour being looked out for and so on. In observational work, it is extremely important to explain what you were looking for and how you decided that what you observed fell into one category or another.

The following information will also be required, but the precise layout and type of information to include will vary from study to study.

- *Observations* How many observations were made? Who was being observed?
- *Observers* How many observers were there? Who were they?
- *Location* Describe the location(s) in which the observations were made. With field observations, describe the location, including important features that might influence the results of the study. Specify how the observations were recorded.
- *Procedure* Explain how the observations were carried out. How did the observers position themselves relative to the observed events? How did the observers ensure that their observations of events were synchronised?

Qualitative studies

Reports of qualitative research studies are written in a slightly different way from quantitative reports. This reflects the very different assumptions and approaches of qualitative and quantitative methods. The format of the report can be adapted according to the precise nature of your research. The guiding principle is to present the information in whichever way produces the clearest, most coherent and least repetitious report.

Remember, always, that the terminology of quantitative research does not sit well (to say the least!) with qualitative approaches. Where an 'experiment' has an 'experimenter', the qualitative 'study' has a 'researcher'. Some qualitative researchers even prefer to call themselves participants too.

The general structure of the qualitative report is the same as that of the quantitative report, in that there is an abstract, introduction, description of the methods used, account of the findings and discussion. However, some of the subsections that are used in quantitative reports do not work well (or at all) in reports of qualitative studies. The key differences are outlined next.

Introduction

As with quantitative reports, the principal purpose of this section is to 'set the scene' for the research and to tell the reader where you were intending to go with this and what you were intending to explore. An explanation of the qualitative methods to be used is also required. Remember, 'qualitative' is not a method in itself, it just presumes a general focus on the study of meaning and interpretation rather than on numbers and comparisons. Include information about the method of data *collection* as well as the method of data *analysis*. For both of these, explain how they are appropriate for exploring your area of interest. Include a statement of the aims of the research study and the research questions.

With some types of qualitative approach, it is sometimes justified not to undertake an extensive literature review prior to collecting and analysing the data. In this case, the review of literature is sometimes included in the discussion rather than the introduction. Do not assume, however, that you can omit a literature review from your introduction with any type of qualitative research. You must make sure that you double-check with your tutor the type of reporting that is appropriate for the qualitative approach and method that you are undertaking.

Method

While qualitative research does not employ the notion of 'replicability', it is still very important that the reader knows precisely how the research was conducted so they are able to judge the quality of the research and its findings. The subsections that you use will depend on the type of study.

Rationale and approach
A brief reiteration of the rationale presented in the introduction. Recap the approach you took and explain why you chose it.

Study design
Explain whether the study consisted of a series of semi-structured interviews, focus groups, a media text study, an observational study, etc. Briefly explain why this method was chosen and relate it to the research questions.

Participants
Detail who took part in the study, how and why they were recruited and their relationship to the researcher. You will need to provide full details about individual participants, as the underlying ethos of qualitative research is that the context in which the research was undertaken is integral to the whole process. Knowing as much as possible about the individual participants is important to fully appreciate the research findings. It is particularly important for the reader to know why those particular people were invited to participate. What was it about them that meant their contribution to the study was anticipated to be useful?

Interviews (or focus groups)
In this section, explain the approach that was taken and describe the interview schedule or focus group schedule and explain how it was developed and what it was designed to achieve.

Procedure

Interviews and focus groups
Here you say exactly how your interviews or focus groups proceeded. Include information about the following.

- Location – where did each session take place?
- For focus groups, the number of people in each group.
- The number of sessions that took place.
- The duration of each session.
- What participants were told before the session began. Include what they were told about the purpose of the session, as well as about their right to withdraw from the study and to anonymity, etc.
- How the session was recorded and what participants were told about this beforehand.
- What participants were told at the end of the session.

Include a reflexive discussion of the impact of the researcher on the scene or setting, how the nature of the task and the interviewer appear to have been understood by participants, whether there were any problems, unforeseen reactions or dilemmas for the researcher. This might also lead into a discussion of any relevant ethical issues that arose. Comment on the interaction between the researcher and the participants and whether, for example, you became aware during the process of trying to elicit specific responses as the session progressed.

Transcription of interviews (or focus groups)
If sessions were audio- or video-recorded, you need to explain how transcription was undertaken. Identify the transcription system that you have used and briefly explain why you chose it. You need to include an explanation of:

- what was transcribed (was everything said by researcher and participant included?)
- whether, and how, pauses, laughter, sighs and other non-verbal sounds were indicated in the transcript
- whether additional notes were made during the session to allow non-verbal behaviour (e.g. facial expressions and gestures) to be included in the transcript and how this was done
- whether, and how, shouting, whispering, tone of voice, etc. were transcribed.

Method of analysis
Explain how you analysed the data. Identify and provide appropriate references for the method that you used (e.g. grounded theory, discourse analysis, IPA). Explain how the analytic approach being used impacts on the interpretation, for example:

The form of discourse analysis that was used was that based upon a model of discursive action (Edwards & Potter, 1992), so it is important to note that the participants' talk around violence and aggression was regarded as interesting in its own right and was not treated as a secondary route to accessing processes, phenomena and events 'beyond' the talk, such as attitudes or cognitive processes.

You also need to explain what you did. For example:

The transcripts were read carefully in order to identify themes that were relevant to the issues being researched. Themes were noted and given titles. Once themes were identified, the transcripts were reread to identify the instances of each of them. Extracts from the transcripts that represented the same theme were grouped together. As the analysis progressed, themes were refined and were regrouped into broader overarching themes...

It is important to explain any decisions that were made while analysing the data (e.g. 'An inclusive approach was taken so that chunks of data only tenuously related to aggression and violence were filed along with those that addressed such issues more directly').

Overall, your Method section should demonstrate that you understand the fundamental principles underlying the style of research that you have adopted.

Analysis/discussion

Note that when you are writing up qualitative research, the data analysis and discussion can be combined to form a single section of the report. The way in which this is presented will, again, depend on the type of method used, as well as the nature of the analysis to be undertaken. Decide whether your report will be clearer if you integrate the analysis and discussion or if it will be more coherent if you keep the two separate.

There are two elements to presenting the data from a qualitative study.

- A description of what the data are like.
- Your analysis and interpretation of what it all means. This is broadly similar to the discussion of the results of a quantitative study, but very different in tone.

Concluding remarks

This separate section is sometimes used to draw everything together at the end of a qualitative report. Incorporate an element of reflexivity. Revisit your overall approach and rationale for carrying out the research. Consider the methods that you used and, with hindsight, whether this was the best way of investigating your research questions. Reflect on your own personal experiences of and feelings about the research process. The reflexive element might include any thoughts you have about the following.

- Your relationship with your participants and your experiences of the research. How did this affect the research process?
- What you expected to find and why (e.g. in terms of your own personal experiences of the topic area). Were these expectations/assumptions borne out?

- Any methodological problems encountered, limitations of the research or issues that these have thrown up and how you might address these if you were to conduct further research.

- How your personal expectations, views and standpoints influenced the way in which you interpreted the data. In qualitative research, remember that subjectivity is to be embraced rather than avoided or denied. It is important to be as clear as possible so that the reader can fully understand where you were coming from when you interpreted your findings.

End with a consideration of what further research could be done and how this would lead on from your findings. Do not suggest using a bigger, more representative sample to make the results more generalisable; leave all that stuff to the quantitative researchers. You might consider whether issues that arose in your study might suggest further research with people from a particular group to explore how they are affected by the issues in question, or you might have identified a specific set of issues that would merit further investigation from a different angle.

Some approaches (e.g. grounded theory) aim to generate testable hypotheses from qualitative work. If your study has used such an approach, make sure that your discussion and concluding remarks are consistent with these aims.

Chapter summary – pulling it all together

→ Can you tick all the points from the revision checklist at the beginning of this chapter?

→ Go to the companion website at www.pearsoned.co.uk/psychologyexpress to access more revision support online, including interactive quizzes, flashcards, You be the marker exercises as well as answer guidance for the Test your knowledge and Sample questions from this chapter.

Further reading for Chapter 11	
Topic	Key reading
Useful guides to developing and reporting research	Scott, J., Koch, R., Scott, G., & Garrison, S. (2002). *The psychology student writer's manual* (2nd ed.). Harlow: Prentice Hall.
	Wood, C., Giles, D., & Percy, C. (2009). *Your psychology project handbook: Becoming a researcher.* Harlow: Pearson.

Explore the accompanying website at www.pearsoned.co.uk/psychologyexpress

→ Prepare more effectively for exams and assignments using the answer guidelines for questions from this chapter.
→ Test your knowledge using multiple choice questions and flashcards.
→ Improve your essay skills by exploring the You be the marker exercises.

Notes

Notes

And finally, before the exam . . .

How to approach revision from here

You should be now at a reasonable stage in your revision process – you should have developed your skills and knowledge base over your course and used this text judiciously over that period. Now, however, you have used the book to reflect, remind and reinforce the material you have researched over the year/ seminar. You will, of course, need to do additional reading and research to that included here (and appropriate directions are provided) but you will be well on your way with the material presented in this book.

It is important that in answering any question in psychology you take a research- and evidence-based approach to your response. For example, do not make generalised or sweeping statements that cannot be substantiated or supported by evidence from the literature. Remember as well that the evidence should not be anecdotal – it is of no use citing your mum, dad, best friend or the latest news from a celebrity website. After all, you are not writing an opinion piece – you are crafting an argument that is based on current scientific knowledge and understanding. You need to be careful about the evidence you present: do review the material and from where it was sourced.

Furthermore, whatever type of assessment you have to undertake, it is important to take an evaluative approach to the evidence. Whether you are writing an essay, sitting an exam or designing a webpage, the key advice is to avoid simply presenting a descriptive answer. Rather, it is necessary to think about the strength of the evidence in each area. One of the key skills for psychology students is critical thinking and for this reason the tasks featured in this series focus upon developing this way of thinking. Thus you are not expected to simply learn a set of facts and figures, but to think about the implications of what we know and how this might be applied in everyday life. The best assessment answers are the ones that take this critical approach.

It is also important to note that psychology is a theoretical subject: when answering any question about psychology, not only refer to the prevailing theories of the field, but also outline the development of them as well. It is also important to evaluate these theories and models either through comparison with other models and theories or through the use of studies that have assessed them and highlighted their strengths and weaknesses. It is essential to read widely – within each section of this book there are directions to interesting and pertinent papers relating to the specific topic area. Find these papers, read these papers and make notes from these papers. But don't stop there. Let them lead you to other sources that may be important to the field. One thing that an examiner hates to see is the same old sources being cited all of the time: be innovative and, as well as reading the seminal works, find the more obscure and interesting sources as well – just make sure they're relevant to your answer!

How not to revise

- **Don't avoid revision.** This is the best tip ever. There is something on the TV, the pub is having a two-for-one offer, the fridge needs cleaning, your budgie looks lonely . . . You have all of these activities to do and they need doing now! Really . . . ? Do some revision!

- **Don't spend too long at each revision session.** Working all day and night is not the answer to revision. You do need to take breaks, so schedule your revision so you are not working from dawn until dusk. A break gives time for the information you have been revising to consolidate.

- **Don't worry.** Worrying will cause you to lose sleep, lose concentration and lose revision time by leaving it late and then later. When the exam comes, you will have no revision completed and will be tired and confused.

- **Don't cram.** This is the worst revision technique in the universe! You will not remember the majority of the information that you try to stuff into your skull, so why bother?

- **Don't read over old notes with no plan.** Your brain will take nothing in. If you wrote your lecture notes in September and the exam is in May is there any point in trying to decipher your scrawly handwriting now?

- **Don't write model answers and learn by rote.** When it comes to the exam you will simply regurgitate the model answer irrespective of the question – not a brilliant way to impress the examiner!

Tips for exam success

What you should do when it comes to revision

Exams are one form of assessment that students often worry about the most. The key to exam success, as with many other types of assessment, lies in good preparation and self-organisation. One of the most important things is knowing what to expect – this does not necessarily mean knowing what the questions will be on the exam paper, but rather what the structure of the paper is, how many questions you are expected to answer, how long the exam will last and so on.

To pass an exam you need a good grasp of the course material and, obvious as it may seem, to turn up for the exam itself. It is important to remember that you aren't expected to know or remember everything in the course, but you should be able to show your understanding of what you have studied. Remember as well that examiners are interested in what you know, not what you don't know. They try to write exam questions that give you a good chance of passing – not ones to catch you out or trick you in any way. You may want to consider some of these top exam tips.

- Start your revision in plenty of time.
- Make a revision timetable and stick to it.
- Practise jotting down answers and making essay plans.
- Practise writing against the clock using past exam papers.
- Check that you have really answered the question and have not strayed off the point.
- Review a recent past paper and check the marking structure.
- Carefully select the topics you are going to revise.
- Use your lecture/study notes and refine them further, if possible, into lists or diagrams and transfer them on to index cards/Post-it notes. Mind maps are a good way of making links between topics and ideas.
- Practise your handwriting – make sure it's neat and legible.

One to two days before the exam
- Recheck times, dates and venue.
- Actively review your notes and key facts.
- Exercise, eat sensibly and get a few good nights' sleep.

On the day
- Get a good night's sleep.
- Have a good meal, two to three hours before the start time.
- Arrive in good time.
- Spend a few minutes calming and focusing.

In the exam room
- Keep calm.
- Take a few minutes to read each question carefully. Don't jump to conclusions – think calmly about what each question means and the area it is focused on.
- Start with the question you feel most confident about. This helps your morale.
- By the same token, don't expend all your efforts on that one question – if you are expected to answer three questions then don't just answer two.
- Keep to time and spread your effort evenly on all opportunities to score marks.
- Once you have chosen a question, jot down any salient facts or key points. Then take five minutes to plan your answer – a spider diagram or a few notes may be enough to focus your ideas. Try to think in terms of 'why and how' not just 'facts'.

- You might find it useful to create a visual plan or map before writing your answer to help you remember to cover everything you need to address.
- Keep reminding yourself of the question and try not to wander off the point.
- Remember that quality of argument is more important than quantity of facts.
- Take 30–60-second breaks whenever you find your focus slipping (typically every 20 minutes).
- Make sure you reference properly – according to your university requirements.
- Watch your spelling and grammar – you could lose marks if you make too many errors.

> **→ Final revision checklist**
>
> ❑ Have you revised the topics highlighted in the revision checklists?
> ❑ Have you attended revision classes and taken note of and/or followed up on your lecturers' advice about the exams or assessment process at your university?
> ❑ Can you answer the questions posed in this text satisfactorily? Don't forget to check sample answers on the website too.
> ❑ Have you read the additional material to make your answer stand out?
> ❑ Remember to criticise appropriately – based on evidence.

Test your knowledge by using the material presented in this text or on the website: **www.pearsoned.co.uk/psychologyexpress**

Glossary

2 × 2 design In an experiment with a '2 × 2 design', there are two independent variables, each with two levels. Each number represents the number of levels in one of the independent variables (so a 3 × 3 design has two independent variables, each with three levels).

acquiescence response bias Acquiescence response bias is the name used to describe the phenomenon where people answering questions, either orally or on paper, get into a habit of saying the same thing over and over again and switch off from thinking about what they are hearing or reading. It can ruin a questionnaire if the questions or items become seemingly predictable.

attitude As McNemar (1946) states, attitudes are invisible. They are a theoretical stance towards a particular subject. When someone expresses an attitude, in speech or writing, that is an opinion. So, our attitude surveys are actually opinion surveys, because that's the data we collect, but because we collect a number of opinions around a construct, we call it an attitude survey. The difference is subtle, but nevertheless exists.

baseline The baseline is the initial measurement of a state before an intervention is applied. It does not mean that nothing is going on; in fact during the baseline a lot of confounding variables are in play, as well as a set of behaviours which you might wish to change using an intervention. Baselines must be measured carefully to ensure that they are stable before proceeding with an intervention.

between-groups design In a between-groups experiment, each participant experiences only one level of the independent variable.

case study A type of narrative account of an individual's personal history used by clinicians.

confounding variable A variable that changes systematically as the independent variable is manipulated (e.g. if an electric fan is used to increase the windiness in a room, the noise level might also increase as the fan works harder). Confounding variables make it difficult to draw clear conclusions about the effects of the independent variable on the dependent variable.

correlation A non-causal relationship between variables.

data Data can take many forms and we should be aware of them. Holliday (2007) lists various types of data in qualitative studies: descriptions of behaviour, of events, of institutions, of appearances, personal narratives, talk, visual records and documents of all types. In quantitative terms, observational data can technically take the form of *any* of these, but converted in some way to some kind of numerical measure, such as the number of times a particular event occurs, rather than a description of it.

demand characteristics The information and cues available to participants in a study that may help them to work out (rightly or wrongly!) the aims of the study and adapt their behaviour accordingly.

dependent variable In an experimental study, the dependent variable is the variable being measured. The purpose of an experiment is to find the effect that manipulating the independent variable has on the dependent variable.

discourse analysis An umbrella term for a range of approaches to qualitative research that involve textual analysis.

ecological validity The extent to which the findings of a study are applicable to everyday life. To have high ecological validity, a study does not necessarily have to be 'realistic'; artificial laboratory studies can have high ecological validity.

experiment A study in which one or more variables is manipulated and the effects measured. Not to be used as a generic term for all types of research study!

experimenter effects The ways in which the behaviour of the experimenter may inadvertently influence the responses of the participants.

field experiment A type of 'quasi-experiment' in which data are collected in a real-world setting, most often without participants being aware that they are taking part.

grounded theory A form of qualitative analysis where the data are used to generate theories, starting from a naive research position.

hypothesis A tentative explanation and prediction about the relationship between variables. Most often used as a systematic prediction of how the results of a study will turn out. Hypotheses are derived from theories.

independent variable In an experimental study, the variable being manipulated by the experimenter is the independent variable. The purpose of an experiment is to find the effect that manipulating the independent variable has on the dependent variable.

informed consent The agreement of participants to take part in a study, based on having been fully informed of the nature, purpose and likely outcomes of a study.

instrument See 'scale'.

interaction In an experimental study with more than one independent variable, an interaction occurs when the effect of one independent variable is different at different levels of another independent variable.

interpretative phenomenological analysis A form of qualitative analysis, predominant in health psychology, centred around understanding and interpreting the world of the individual as they experience it.

interpretative repertoire A repertoire is a particular set of words or phrases or ways of expression, such as tones of voice, which is used in a particular context by a particular person. You might notice in a transcript that whenever someone refers to their own behaviour or ideas they say 'kind of' or 'sort of', but when they refer to someone else they say 'do you know what I mean?' This might be worth noting and certainly could be characterised as part of a repertoire. 'Kind of' and 'sort of' are phrases that one might read as an expression of doubt or vagueness, whereas 'do you know what I mean?' could express a questioning of the other speaker. In one case, the person questions themselves, in another case they question the interviewer, for example.

Latin square A method of counterbalancing orders of conditions using a subset of all possible orders. In a Latin square, each item occurs exactly once in each of the possible positions in the sequence.

Likert scaling A form of response scaling involving fixed points on a continuum given meaningful verbal labels – for example, 'agree strongly', 'agree', 'neither agree nor disagree', 'disagree' and 'disagree strongly'.

mixed design A type of experiment in which there is more than one independent variable, including at least one between-groups and one within-groups variable.

natural experiment A type of 'quasi-experiment' in which the experimenter makes use of naturally occurring conditions rather than manipulating an independent variable.

operational definition The definition of a concept in terms of how it can be measured (e.g. an operational definition of 'happiness' might be how much someone smiles during a three-minute conversation).

opinion See 'attitude'.

participant observation A form of data collection that involves the researcher posing as or becoming a member of a social or other group for the purposes of developing special insights.

quasi-experiment In a quasi-experiment, comparisons are made between levels of an independent variable, but the manipulation of the variables does not satisfy the conditions for being a 'true' experiment.

random A situation in which every possible outcome has an equal chance of occurring.

rationale The rationale for a research study is a coherent explanation of the reasons for conducting the study, what it is based on and what is expected or hoped to be achieved.

reliability The consistency and stability of a measure, either within itself (internal reliability) or over time (external reliability).

sampling bias Sampling bias occurs when participants have been selected in such a way that it has a systematic effect on the outcome of a study.

saturation In qualitative research, the point at which analysis of the data yields no new themes or ideas.

scale (instrument) The word 'scale' is used in two different ways. Scale is often used to mean the whole thing that you give to people – for example, a stress scale. This is synonymous with 'instrument' or 'test'. However, when you respond to an item within a scale, you do so using a scale (such as a Likert scale or a visual analogue scale). Using the terms 'instrument', 'item' and 'scale' prevents confusion. After all, a scale is a thing you use to measure with, not the thing itself.

single-case design A form of research with an experimental framework applied to a single individual.

stopping rules Rules for deciding when to stop conducting research, usually set up for ethical reasons.

thematic analysis A form of qualitative analysis that is commonly used in health (but not health psychology) research and is focused on deriving themes from data appearing most commonly in transcripts. It is a quicker and less resource-intensive method than other methods commonly used by psychologists.

theory A logically organised set of claims or statements that serves to explain observed phenomena and the relationships between them. Good theories describe, explain and predict phenomena. Hypotheses derived from theories can be directly tested.

validity The extent to which a measure is actually measuring what it is supposed to be measuring.

within-groups design In a within-groups experiment, each participant experiences all levels of the independent variable. This is not to be confused with a correlational study in which multiple measures are taken from participants but nothing is manipulated.

References

Allport, G. W. (1937). *Personality*. New York: Holt.

Beelman, W., & Schmidt-Denter, U. (2009). Mother–child interaction following marital separation: A longitudinal observation study. *European Psychologist, 14*, 307–319.

BPS (2004). *Guidelines for minimum standards of ethical approval in psychological research*. Leicester: British Psychological Society.

BPS (2007). *Guidelines for psychologists working with animals*. Leicester: British Psychological Society.

BPS (2009). *Code of ethics and conduct*. Leicester: British Psychological society.

Glaser, B. G., & Strauss, A. L. (1967). *The discovery of grounded theory: Strategies for qualitative research*. Chicago, IL: Aldine.

Godden, D. R., & Baddeley, A. D. (1975). Context-dependent memory in two natural environments: On land and underwater. *British Journal of Psychology, 66*(3), 325–331.

Godden, D. R., & Baddeley, A. D. (1980). When does context influence recognition memory? *British Journal of Psychology, 71*(1), 99–104.

Harré, R. (2004). Staking our claim for qualitative psychology as science. *Qualitative Research in Psychology, 1*(1), 3–14.

Holliday, A. (2007). *Doing and writing qualitative research* (2nd ed.). London: Sage.

Huber, J. W., Taffinder, N. N., Russell, R. G., & Darzi, A. A. (2003). The effects of different viewing conditions on performance in simulated minimal access surgery. *Ergonomics, 46*(10), 999–1016.

Humphreys, L. (1970). *Tearoom trade: A study of homosexual encounters in public places*. London: Duckworth.

Hurlbert, A. C., & Ling, Y. (2007). Biological components of sex differences in color preference. *Current Biology, 17*(16), R623–R625.

Ittenbach, R. F., & Lawhead, W. F. (1996). Historical and philosophical foundations of single-case research. In R. D. Franklin, D. B. Allison & B. S. Gorman (Eds.), *Design and analysis of single-case research*. Mahwah, New Jersey: Lawrence Erlbaum.

Kenealy, P. (1997). Mood-state-dependent retrieval: The effects of induced mood on memory reconsidered. *The Quarterly Journal of Experimental Psychology Section A: Human Experimental Psychology, 50*(2), 290–317.

Knudson, R. M. (2006). Anorexia dreaming: A case study. *Dreaming, 16*, 43–52.

Likert, R. (1932). A technique for the measurement of attitudes. *Archives of Psychology, 22*(140), 1–55.

Macintosh, K., & Dissanayake, C. (2006). A comparative study of the spontaneous social interactions of children with high-functioning autism and children with Asperger's disorder. *Autism, 10*(2), 199–220.

McNemar, Q. (1946). Opinion–attitude methodology. *Psychological Bulletin, 43*, 289–374.

Milgram, S. (1963). Behavioral study of obedience. *The Journal of Abnormal and Social Psychology, 67*(4), 371–378.

North, A. C., Hargreaves, D. J., & McKendrick, J. (1999). The influence of in-store music on wine selections. *Journal of Applied Psychology, 84*(2), 271–276.

Osgood, C. E., Suci, G., & Tannenbaum, P. (1957). *The measurement of meaning*. Urbana, IL: University of Illinois Press.

Parker, I. (1992). *Discourse dynamics: Critical analysis for social and individual psychology*. New York: Routledge.

Popper, K. (1959). *The logic of scientific discovery*. New York: Basic Books.

References

Potter, J., & Wetherell, M. (1987). *Discourse and social psychology: Beyond attitudes and behaviour.* London: Sage.

QAA (2010). *Quality Assurance Agency benchmark for psychology.* London: Quality Assurance Agency.

Raaijmakers, Q. A. W., Van Hoof, A., 't Hart, H., Verbogt, T. F. M. A., & Vollebergh, W. A. M. (2000). Adolescents' midpoint responses on Likert-type scale items: Neutral or missing values? *International Journal of Public Opinion Research, 12,* 208–217.

Schraw, G., Wadkins, T., & Olafson, L. (2007). Doing the things we do: A grounded theory study of academic procrastination. *Journal of Educational Psychology, 99,* 12–25.

Shapiro, C. J., Smith, B. H., Malone, P. S., & Collaro, A. L. (2010). Natural experiment in deviant peer exposure and youth recidivism. *Journal of Clinical Child & Adolescent Psychology, 39*(2), 242–251.

Sidman, M. (1960). *Tactics of scientific research.* New York: Basic Books.

Smith, J., Jarman, M., & Osborne, M. (1999). Doing interpretative phenomenological analysis. In M. Murray & K. Chamberlain (Eds.), *Qualitative health psychology.* London: Sage.

Thurstone, L. L., & Chave, E. J. (1929). *The measurement of attitude.* Chicago, IL: University of Chicago Press.

Wiederman, M. (1999). Volunteer bias in sexuality research using college student participants. *Journal of Sex Research, 36*(1), 59–66.

Wilson, T. D., Lindsey, S., & Schooler, T. Y. (2000). A model of dual attitudes. *Psychological Review, 107,* 101–126.

Wood, B. T., Worthington, Jr., E. L., Juola Exline, J., Yali, A. M., Aten, J. D., & McMinn, M. R. (2010). Development, refinement, and psychometric properties of the Attitudes Toward God Scale (ATGS-9). *Psychology of Religion and Spirituality, 2,* 148–167.

Index

Note: Page entries in **bold** refer to terms defined in the Glossary